OCCUPATION AND CAREER EDUCATION LEGISLATION

Second Edition

Dennis C. Nystrom, Ed.D.
   Dean, Division of Career Education
   Rochester Institute of Technology

G. Keith Bayne, Ph.D.
   Department of Occupational and
      Career Education
   University of Louisville

Bobbs-Merrill Educational Publishing
Indianapolis

Dedicated to
Preservice and Inservice Occupation
and Career Education Professionals

The Bobbs-Merrill Company, Inc.
4300 West 62nd Street
Indianapolis, Indiana 46268

Second Edition
First Printing 1979

Library of Congress Cataloging in Publication Data

Nystrom, Dennis C.
    Occupation and career education legislation.

    Bibliography: p.
    1. Vocational education—Law and legislation—United States. 2. Career education—Law and legislation—United States. I. Bayne, G. Keith, joint author.
II. Title.
KF4205.Z9N95   1979   344'.73'077   79-12548
ISBN 0-672-97133-X

Preface

It is always a pleasure for an author to be preparing the preface to the second edition of a book. That usually means that the first edition has had enough market appeal to have sold a sizeable number of copies. We are not absolutely certain, however, that the second edition of *Occupation and Career Education* is being produced because of huge sales volume. The law is always changing, and that is the main factor that calls for frequent revisions in a book on legislation. To those of you who have asked for a new edition that looks at recent legislation, we thank you.

Before discussing some of the new components of this book, we would like to offer a few words of caution and concern. These considerations focus on the relationship of federal legislation to professional philosophy. In the areas of occupational and career education, it is often too easy to confuse policy dictated by federal legislation with educational philosophy that may or may not serve as the underlying theme of the legislation.

At a national conference conducted in Nashville, Tennessee, from March 8 through March 10, 1977, over one hundred selected professionals met to discuss educational philosophy. This group, composed of occupational and career education professionals, state and national advisory groups, federal and state administrators, philosophers, and others, identified a major concern related to occupational and career education. That concern was that we in the profession may have become so accustomed to programming based on legislative policy that we may have neglected to apply a strong professional philosophy to our endeavors. Therefore, it is important to remember that professional philosophy must be a crucial component of legislation and programming, and that legislation may have an impact on professional philosophy. Never, however, must legislative policy be mistaken for a sound philosophical base.

The second edition of *Occupation and Career Education* has been expanded to include new legislation and recent amendments. Following is a description of the modifications included in this edition.

Chapter 5 now includes a detailed analysis of the Comprehensive Employment and Training Act. CETA plays a significant role in the total system of occupational and career education.

The Education Amendments of 1974 have been added to chapter 6. These amendments represent a continued progression toward a single, consolidated educational enactment.

Chapter 7 details the new and exciting Education Amendments of 1976. Particular emphasis has been placed on the career education, vocational education, and student financial assistance categories.

Chapter 8 looks at legislation supporting career education for the handicapped. Particular emphasis has been placed on Public Law 94-142.

The Equal Employment Opportunity Act is the topic of chapter 9. Preservice and inservice program administrators will find this chapter particularly useful.

We sincerely hope that you will find the second edition of *Occupation and Career Education* a useful tool in teaching, managing, and coordinating occupational and career education programs. If it helps you, the preservice and inservice professional, to better serve your students, then the effort expended in its preparation has been worth it.

D. C. N.

G. K. B.

Contents

Introduction

Although the classic curriculum has tended to deal more with educational philosophy than with educational legislation and although students traditionally prefer such emphasis, federal and state legislation has had more impact on the development of formal education in the United States than all the Rousseaus, Herbarts, and Deweys combined. Philosophies—educational, social, and otherwise—may inspire new movements; but, usually, it is the legislation that establishes the environmental conditions under which these movements will be developed and applied.

The "antilegislation syndrome" (characteristically found alike in the greenest undergraduate and the most experienced graduate student) apparently is based upon the concept that legislative subject matter is boring and irrelevant. For example, an in-depth analysis of the sections and subsections of the Smith-Hughes Act appears relatively insignificant when contrasted with the vast scheme of today's career education and, studied in isolation, it is. The real importance of any historical legislative enactment exists in its relation to the national condition at the time of its passage and in its effect on contemporary and future legislation.

Any occupational program manager or educator can attest to the fact that knowledge of specific legislation relating to his or her career education programs is essential. In most states, various administrative agencies provide consultive services of this type to the public schools. The real problem, as these same people will verify, is in determining intermediate- and long-range program goals when current legislative enactments and their administrative procedures are sure to change. The individual program planner must have the ability to make these projections. The real value in studying legislation, both past and present, is not in memorizing the sections and subsections of the various laws, but rather in being able to predict future trends and to utilize these predictions in the program planning function. The study of legislation must be based on a systematically structured framework that permits analysis of all factors leading to the passage and administration of an Act. The learning relative to legislation must be in the affective domain. Verbs such as discuss, analyze, differentiate, synthesize, and verify must be indicative of legislative study.

Key Factors Affecting Legislation

In order to predict future trends, the planner must be able to determine those key factors or elements around which legislation is generated and enactments administered. Any legislation occurs within an historical context, and every legislative bill must have a cause. The authors have identified four major factors that are responsible for legislative enactments. These factors must be analyzed, not only individually, but in concert with one another. They are listed below in alphabetical order, rather than in any order of importance:

1. Economic factors
2. Political factors
3. Professional factors
4. Social factors

Economic factors, such as the great depression of the 1930s, the recession of the 1950s and the most recent economic turmoil, have been responsible for many major enactments. The early westward movement, Roosevelt's National Reconstruction Act, and much of the Office of Economic Opportunity (OEO) enabling legislation also have been based on various economic conditions that existed both across the nation and within target groups.

Political factors, such as the extended war in Vietnam, Watergate, and international relations, are probably the most significant causes of legislative enactments, but it is virtually impossible to separate the political aspects from any of the other three factors when analyzing legislation. Individual personalities also play a significant political part in any legislative enactment.

Professional factors, such as an increasing concern for career education, are also significant causes of legislative reform. Inputs of individual professionals and their organizations are certainly considered when drafting new bills. Probably of greater importance is the professionals' interpretation of specific legislation after it becomes law. National, state, and local-level administrators can greatly affect the specific character of funding procedures.

Social factors, such as civil disobedience, an increasing crime rate in our large metropolitan areas, and a decrease in public concern for general educational programs, are underlying themes for all legislative change and adoption. As with all the other factors, it is extremely difficult to pinpoint any single aspect of the social structure as a contributor to a bill's introduction and passage. However, general social trends can be analyzed and related to legislation. Recent emphasis on humanitarianism, brought about by emerging psychological schools of thought as well as by other factors, certainly is reflected in new legislation and recent legal decisions.

When studied from this historical frame of reference, legislation can be meaningful and interesting. This approach to legislative analysis changes learning from a cognitive process to an affective one. The old memorization game no longer is relevant when the study of legislation is related to an overall goal of being able to predict future trends to make the future planning process realistic.

This approach also overcomes another traditional problem associated with teaching legislation, i.e., materials utilized do not become dated so quickly, since the specific act itself is relegated to a relatively low level of significance. Rather, it is the reason for its passage, the trends that existed at that time, the factors that led to its administration, and its influence on current or pending legislation that are important.

This book treats the study of occupational and career legislation as both a cognitive and affective process. It is concerned with the "whys" and the "wherefores," rather than the "whats." It is designed to provide necessary skills to the reader, so that he or she may interpret cultural and social events in a formal context around which predictions regarding future legislative enactments and their outcomes can be made.

Self-Study Model

Each chapter is designed as a separate unit of study consisting of objectives, introductory material, certain references, questions for review, and suggested activities. This format should be equally effective for either classroom instruction or self-study. Each unit or chapter should require from five to six hours to complete (except for the suggested activities section).

Chapter objectives are designed to guide the learner through the introductory material and several of the suggested references. It is assumed that some of the suggested reading material already will have been read.

The questions and suggested activities at the end of each chapter will require more than merely rote responses from the introductory information and the suggested references. Through analysis of the aforementioned material, the student will be asked to make inferences regarding the various causal factors and implications of the various enactments.

This higher level learning process is the goal of this book. Certainly, there is much more to any legislative act than the bill itself. The reasons for its existence, the success with which it dealt with some cultural need, and the effect it has had on contemporary programs and legislation are the important factors associated with any enactment.

1

What Is Legislation ?

Objectives

- The student will describe the legislative process from the stimulus/response frame of reference.
- The student will define the various levels at which interpretive procedures can affect the outcomes of a legislative enactment.
- The student will differentiate between authorizations and appropriations as they refer to the various legislative enactments.

Introduction

Legislation is a process. It is a process in which some cultural need is identified, interpreted, and dealt with. The major problem associated with this legislative process is that all levels from the essential cultural need through the administration of an enactment are tainted by various interpretive procedures. The legislative process is diagrammed in Fig. 1-1.

As illustrated in Fig. 1-1, the stimulus that eventually precipitates a legislative enactment may be far removed from the response that comes about through the legislative process. Hence, while a cause-and-effect relationship certainly exists, much of the effect grows out of matters extrinsic to the cause. It is, therefore, important that students of legislation, in any area, be familiar with all facets of the process and their implications for the end result—a workable response to an identified need.

Cultural Need (Stimulus)

Any legislative enactment, whether it is in occupation education or in internal revenue, grows out of an identified cultural need. Generally speaking, these needs may be found in one or more of the previously discussed areas, i.e., economic, political, professional, and/or social realms. This need is usually identified to a member of Congress from any number of sources; the most common sources are constituent letters, lobby groups, administrative personnel, or other governmental agencies.

Fig. 1-1. The Legislative Process

Oftentimes, it is evident that cultural or societal needs may be interpreted differently by different groups. For example, many health professionals feel that fluoridated water is essential for healthy teeth and that the federal government should pass legislation requiring all cities and municipalities to provide fluoridated water to their residents. On the other hand, some private-interest groups are strongly opposed to such tactics on the basis of their being "unnatural" or "Communistic." Likewise, many occupational educators feel that vocational training can best be accomplished through the public schools, while others believe that private agencies should have the control.

Hence, it is plain to see that even in the identification of need, much controversy exists. Before a bill can even be introduced by a congressional representative of the people, several factors must be taken into consideration. The desires of the constituency must be considered, as well as its real knowledge of the problem at hand; also, the representative's political interactions and future as well as personal beliefs and interests.

Conservation and environment are topics in which everyone is interested. The majority of Americans are concerned with preserving the environment, but how it should be done certainly is open to debate. Every legislator knows that to support selective harvesting of wildlife will offend some constituents and that to eliminate public hunting will offend others.

Thus, it is clear that the identification of cultural need is fraught with many levels of interpretation. From the stimulus—response frame of reference—the stimulus is, at best, poorly defined.

Pre-Legislative Manipulation

Supposing a member of Congress reaches a decision regarding a definite need for a bill and prepares a rough draft to the proposed enactment based on his or her understanding of the problem. It is clear that this understanding may vary somewhat from the specific input of the representative's constituency. The rough draft of the bill is then sent to the Legislative Reference Service. This unit within the Library of Congress writes a legal bill based on the legislator's draft. Of course, various legal requirements of a bill and even its format may slightly alter its initial intent.

At this point, after receiving more input from various sources, the representative may elect either to discard the bill or to schedule it for its first reading on the floor of Congress. This decision is based on political pressures, constituency support, whether a similar proposal already has been introduced, and administrative support. If the bill is read, the presiding officer of the house of Congress will refer the bill to a committee via the parliamentarian. The committee to which a bill is assigned can very well spell either life or death for that bill.

After the bill is assigned to a committee, it will be directed to a subcommittee whose task is to gather pertinent information regarding the bill. When all the information regarding a bill has been gathered, the staff of the subcommittee draws up various reports regarding the bill. These reports often reflect the political affiliation of the staff members. The partisan reports are then discussed and compromises are made. The bill is then forwarded to the subcommittee chair, who will slate it for reading to the committee as a whole. If the chair does not favor the proposed legislation, he or she can kill the bill by preventing the whole committee from reviewing it. A bill can, however, be called up from committee.

After the bill is presented to the committee, debate, further hearings, and amendments are in order. If the bill survives these tests, it may be ordered to printing and then distributed to the entire house in which it was introduced.

However, the bill still is not ready for debate and vote. It must be presented to the Rules Committee. This very powerful committee determines the method by which the bill may be considered and amended. The Rules Committee also determines a date when the bill can be read and the amount of time for debate. In effect then, the Rules Committee can destroy the chances for a bill to pass.

If, after all of this, the bill finally arrives on the floor of Congress, it is open for debate. In most cases, there is very little debate, and the bill is voted upon. If it passes, it is referred to the other house of the Congress, where similar actions already may have taken place; or it will be implemented at the committee and subcommittee level. The real difficulty at this point is to get the bill voted upon by the other house of the Congress.

The general nature of the House of Representatives during the Ninety-second Congress might best be described as conservative when related to the rather liberal Senate of that same Congress. It is clear to see that regardless of which way a legislative bill travels—from House to Senate or from Senate to House—it is in for considerable scrutiny in the other chamber of the Congress. Once again, the bill must overcome another major hurdle. Getting the second chamber to vote on the bill or preventing them from "amending it to death" is a difficult task at best.

Supposing the bill is voted upon and approved by the second chamber, it is then ready to move to the Conference Committee. This private committee meeting is used to compromise the differences between the two versions of the bill. Once the compromised bill is completed, it is sent to both houses of Congress for a vote. Only the final draft is voted upon; no amendments or deletions may be included.

At last the bill has either passed or failed! If passed, another bill becomes law. The Chief Executive, the President of the United States, must sign the bill into law. The President's political ambitions as well as the input from advisors will temper his or her response to any legislative enactment. A President certainly can spell either life or death for an act, since such a large majority vote is required of both houses of Congress to override a presidential veto. Once his or her signature is affixed to a bill, however, it becomes law. However, this specific law still must undergo several levels of interpretation. At this point, we will focus our discussion on occupational or career education legislation, since other types of laws are interpreted by different agencies.

Post-Legislative Interpretation

With few exceptions, the fact that a law exists does not guarantee that monies provided for in its various titles will be available. In other words, monies can be authorized by various legislative enactments, but no guarantee can be made regarding their appropriation. A good example of this type of action is Part E, Section 151 (b), of the Vocational Education Amendments (VEA) of 1968. Ninety million dollars were authorized for the construction of residential vocational schools for the 1969, 1970, and 1971 fiscal years; but no money was appropriated for this particular part of the Act. Hence, there has been no construction of residential schools funded under the VEA '68. On the other hand, the Smith-Hughes Act was an automatic appropriation enactment.

Even more important than this authorization/appropriation syndrome associated with educational legislation are the levels of interpretation that each section of the enactment must go through. After a bill is passed and money is appropriated, the central administrative office (in the case of education legislation—U.S. Office of Education (USOE) must determine just how the money is to be spent within the guidelines of the Act. In most cases, the Act is quite flexible and open for considerable interpretation. Hence, various administrative offices within USOE develop guidelines for the states in order to provide them some direction in spending.

In most cases, these federal guidelines that are provided to the states also are flexible. As a result, the various state administrative agencies provide their own interpretation of the federal directives and give this information to the local school districts. Once again, each local school district interprets the state guidelines when they administer the funds to their programs. Finally, program directors and local teachers have some degree of flexibility in spending the federal funds.

Program Nature

The resultant educational programs may vary as much as there are different people administering them. In summation, is it any wonder that there are as many different occupational programs as there are school districts and instructors in the country? Also, it is quite possible that the resulting programs in no way account for the identified cultural need that was the stimulus for the enactment.

Questions for Review

1. How does a congressional representative receive information regarding the need for an enactment?

2. What is the common name of the rough draft of a bill that is prepared by a member of Congress?

3. What is the function of the Conference Committee?

4. Differentiate between authorizations and appropriations. What famous vocational education act was an automatic appropriation enactment?

Suggested Activities

1. Design a general letter format that could be used to inform a congressional representative about certain concerns.

2. Describe a coordinated procedure that could be utilized to inform a member of Congress about the feelings of large groups of people

regarding needed or unneeded legislation. Prepare a procedure for:

   a. Local community
   b. Local school personnel
   c. Professional organization members.

3. Prepare a listing of your state's members of the House of Representatives and Senate. Also prepare a listing of state-level representatives.

4. Analyze the legislative process and prepare a paper describing the levels at which local constituents can have the greatest influence on an enactment.

5. Contact your congressional representative and request information on the best way to get in touch with him or her regarding various legislative proposals and enactments.

Notes and Revisions

2

Early Legislation: *The Foundations of Occupational Education*

Objectives

- The student will review information concerned with the various legislative enactments of this period.
- The student will describe those economic, political, professional, and social factors leading to the passage of the following acts.
- The student will describe the effects these legislative enactments have had on current occupational education programs.

Introduction

Early occupational education legislation may be defined as those enactments beginning with the Morrill Act of 1862 and extending to the Health Amendments to the George-Barden Act in 1956. During the early period, there were three major eras in which considerable legislation was passed.

The early period, the late 1800s and early 1900s, was characterized by a major westward expansion. The need for skilled people in agriculture was especially evident. The success of our westward growth depended primarily on the ability of the pioneers to "stick it out." This meant that the primary emphasis was on fulfilling the basic physiological needs. Food, clothing, and shelter came from agricultural or biological sources, hence, the importance placed on these areas in the early legislation.

The second period was around the time of World War I. The war effort and necessity for skilled personnel at home demonstrated the necessity for federal support of vocational education. The increasing industrialization of the country also was responsible for massive manpower shortages that could only be filled by skilled personnel.

The third period is somewhat more strung out than the second. Once again, the constantly increasing industrialization caused manpower shortages. An ever-increasing population also was responsible for much-needed agricultural advancements. Of course, the Great Depression of the 1930s also was instrumental in causing increased legislation aimed at putting people to work.

A brief analysis of the specific acts involved may be helpful.

Morrill Act 1862

The Morrill Act, named after the honorable Justin A. Morrill (Senator) from Vermont, provided each state with 30,000 acres of public land for each Senator and Representative in Congress. This land was to be used for the establishment of agricultural colleges in each state. The primary purpose of the Act was to provide the major part of instruction in the agricultural and mechanical arts. This Act is significant in that it was the first aid granted by the federal government specifically for vocational education, even though its proponents were not fully aware of that fact.

Second Morrill Act 1890

In 1890, Congress passed the Second Morrill Act. This Act granted $1,500 annually plus a $1,000 automatic increase each year for support of the colleges created by the Morrill Act of 1862.

Nelson Amendment 1907

The Nelson Amendment provided an additional sum of money based on a sliding scale each year for further support of the agricultural colleges established by the original Morrill Act. The Nelson Amendment provided funding categories for teacher training in the agricultural and mechanical arts.

Smith-Lever Act 1914

Senator Hoke Smith of Georgia and Representative Lever of South Carolina introduced a bill to establish extension training programs in agriculture and home economics. This bill became law in 1914 and is known as the Smith-Lever Act. Because of certain political tradeoffs used to secure passage of the Smith-Lever Act, President Wilson was authorized to appoint a commission to examine the need for federal support to aid vocational education. This commission, called the Commission on National Aid to Vocational Education, studied the need of vocational education at the state level and the role federal legislation could play in providing a national system of vocational education. The report of the Commission led to the passage of the Smith-Hughes Act.

Smith-Hughes Act 1917

The Smith-Hughes Act was probably the single most important legislative enactment aimed at vocational education until the passage of the Vocational Education Act of 1963 and the 1968 Vocational Education Amendments. Most of the structure of vocational education today is a result of the Smith-Hughes Act, even though nearly a decade of new legislation has existed regarding vocational education.

The Smith-Hughes Act automatically appropriated 7.2 million dollars annually to the states on the basis of their rural, urban, and total population proportions. The money was provided to the states on a 50-50 matching basis for vocational education in agriculture, home economics, and trade and industry. The addition of the trade and industry category was a result of the **Report of the Commission on National Aid to Vocational Education.**

The Act was administered by a Federal Board of Vocational Education which was responsible directly to the Congress. The Federal Board consisted of the Secretary of Labor, Secretary of Agriculture, Secretary of Commerce, U.S. Commissioner of Education, and three presidentially appointed citizens. The Federal Board was granted $200,000 annually for its operation.

To receive federal monies for vocational education, each state was required to submit an annual plan prepared by a State Board of Vocational Education. This State Board was to be the administrative body in each state for vocational education at the state level.

Smith-Sears Act 1918

The Smith-Sears Act passed on June 27, 1918, authorized funds for retraining programs designed to help returning disabled soldiers and sailors from World War I.

Smith-Bankhead Act 1920

The Smith-Bankhead Act, better known as the Federal Rehabilitation Act, was approved on June 2, 1920. It provided for the vocational rehabilitation of disabled persons to return to civil employment. Unlike the Smith-Sears Act, this enactment was aimed at the disabled civilian employee. It provided for a special **rehabilitation board** in each state and Assistant Director for Vocational Rehabilitation in charge of the administration of the Act at the federal level.

George-Reed Act 1929

The George-Reed Act was a short-term supplemental authorization enactment which provided a total of $2,500,000 over a five-year period. The money authorized by this Act was for home economics and agricultural education in the states. No additional funds were authorized in the Act for trade and industrial education.

George-Ellzey Act 1934

The George-Ellzey Act also was a short-term supplemental authorization enactment passed to replace the George-Reed Act, which terminated on June 30, 1934. This Act authorized $3 million annually for each of three years. Unlike the George-Reed Act, the George-Ellzey Act provided funds for trade and industrial education, as well as agricultural education and home economics education.

George-Deen Act 1936

The George-Deen Act was approved by Congress and signed into law on June 8, 1936. The Act became effective on July 1, 1937. This also was a supplemental authorization bill like its forerunners, the George-Reed and the George-Ellzey Acts. The Act authorized 12 million annually to be divided among agricultural, home economics, and trade and industrial education. Money also was authorized for distributive education and teacher education programs.

The significance of the George-Deen Act was that it recognized that the personal and public service occupations also required skilled people. Vocational education began to broaden its scope.

George-Barden Act 1946

The Vocational Education Act of 1946, better known as the George-Barden Act, represented a major amendment to the George-Deen Act and an even more flexible enactment than its predecessor. The George-Barden Act was, in effect, a supplemental authorization to the Smith-Hughes Act. Therefore, its administrative procedures were much the same as previous enactments.

The authorization of the Act totaled in excess of $28,850,000 annually for agricultural, home economics, trade and industrial, and distributive education. Also included in the authorization were funds for the administrative costs incurred by the Office of Education and for vocational education in the fishery trades.

The George-Barden Act provided greater state-level control in the utilization of appropriated funds. For example, there were no specific allocations for teacher training; however, it was up to the state boards to determine the allotment for this function. Hence, from the George-Deen Act through the George-Barden Act and onward to the '63 and '68 Acts, the trend toward vocational education funding flexibility continued.

Health Amendment, George-Barden Act 1956

The Health Amendments Act of 1956, better known as the George-Barden Health Amendment, provided funds for practical-nurse training.

Fishery Amendment, George-Barden Act 1956

Congress approved a $375,000 appropriation as an amendment to the George-Barden Act to promote the fishing industry, as well as the distribution aspects of commercial fishing. The appropriations, as a result of this authorization, were to be equally divided among the states and territories—based on the size of their fishing industry. The U.S. Commissioner of Education and the Secretary of the Interior would determine how the appropriations were to be divided.

Summary

There is little question that the earliest of the legislative enactments aimed at promoting vocational education have had, and still have, the greatest effect on occupational education programs. Many of the programs that grew out of the Smith-Hughes and George-Barden Acts remain virtually unchanged today. As strange as it may seem, many of these programs are still quite relevant and are providing realistic vocational training opportunities for today's youth.

Questions for Review

1. Why were the very early vocational education legislative enactments aimed at training primarily in the agricultural- and home economics-related occupations?

2. What effects did the early development of trade unions and their respective legislative guides have on the legislation for vocational education of this period?

3. Why was trade and industrial education not included in the George-Reed Act?

4. Is there a correlation between major wars and legislation for vocational education? Why?

5. What effect, if any, did the economic depression of the 1930s have on vocational education legislation affecting home economics, agriculture, and trades and industry?

Suggested Activities

1. Prepare a paper discussing the role and function of the Commission on National Aid to Vocational Education.

2. Develop a time line of federal legislative enactments. Analyze the various groupings that occur.

3. Prepare a short legislative biography of the Honorable Justin A. Morrill, Senator from Vermont. Compare and contrast his legislative life with a contemporary occupational education legislator.

4. Prepare a graph depicting the amount of money authorized for vocational education during the early period. Make the graph large enough that it can be expanded as later enactments are studied.

5. Compare and contrast the legislative authorizations for vocational education with the population at the time of passage of the various enactments. What conclusions can be drawn regarding the per capita expenditures for vocational education?

Bibliography

"Administration of the Smith-Hughes Act," *School and Society* 6 (November 17, 1917): 594.

Barlow, Melvin L. *History of Industrial Education in the United States.* Peoria, Ill.: Bennett, 1967.

Bennett, Charles A. *History of Manual and Industrial Education up to 1870.* Peoria, Ill.: Bennett, 1926.

Drayer, Adam. *The Teacher in a Democratic Society.* Columbus, Ohio: Merrill, 1970.

"Federal Aid Limited to Vocational Training," *Industrial Arts and Vocational Education,* February 1931.

Fite, Gilbert C., and Jim E. Reese. *An Economic History of the U.S.* Boston: Houghton Mifflin, 1970.

Hawkins, Layton S., et. al. *Development of Vocational Education.* Chicago: American Technical Society, 1951.

"History of Federal Funds for Vocational Education," *American Vocations,* December 1956.

McCarthy, John. *Vocational Education: America's Greatest Resource*. Chicago: American Technical Society, 1951.

McGivern, Gregory James. *First Hundred Years of Engineering Education in the United States (1807-1907)*. Spokane: Gonzaga University Press, 1962.

Morrison, Samuel E., and Henry Steele Commanger. *The Growth of the American Republic*. New York: Oxford University Press, 1962.

"Need for Vocational Education," *School and Society* 37 (June 16, 1933): 754.

"New George-Barden Vocational Education Act," *Industrial Arts and Vocational Education*, November 1946.

"Provisions of George-Barden Vocational Education Act," *Agricultural Magazine*, December 1946.

Roberts, Roy W. *Vocational and Practical Arts Education*. New York: Harper, 1965.

Struck, F. Theodore. *Vocational Education for a Changing World*. New York: Wiley, 1945.

Venn, Grant. *Man, Education and Work*. Washington, D.C.: American Council on Education, 1964.

Notes and Revisions

3

The Sputnik Crisis: *How to Obtain a Technical Surplus Without Really Trying*

Objectives

- The students will review information concerned with the various legislative enactments and their amendments that grew out of the Sputnik era.
- The students will describe those economic, political, professional, and social factors leading to the passage of the aforementioned enactments.
- The students will describe the effects these legislative enactments have had on current occupational educational programs.
- The students will analyze current manpower data to determine the strength and weaknesses of the educational legislation of the Sputnik era.

Introduction

The "go to college" syndrome was never stronger than during the latter days of 1958 through the middle 1960s. The success of the USSR in its space program, as demonstrated in the successful launching of Sputnik, made Americans realize their relative status with regard to other countries in the technical and scientific areas. Like other periods in our nation's history, the crisis legislation began pouring out of Congress. Huge manpower shortages in electronics, aerospace engineering, mathematics, and foreign languages were cited as weak spots in our previous educational programs.

The National Defense Education Act (NDEA) of 1958 typifies the thrust of most legislation passed during this period. It stressed science, mathematics, foreign language, and technical competencies. Also, it provided huge sums of money for postgraduate training in these areas. There is little doubt that this piece of legislation has had a greater impact on traditional education programs at all levels than any other single enactment.

Several other enactments of this era also are significant. Following is a listing and brief summary of these laws.

National Defense Education Act (NDEA) 1958

The effects of the NDEA of 1958 on occupational education programs are often overlooked. In most cases, occupational or vocational educators concern themselves only with study of Title VIII of that Act which was an amendment to Title III of the earlier George-Barden Act. The enactment of this law in September of 1958 made possible an annual appropriation of $15 million for the operation of vocational training programs in area vocational schools in each state.

Funds under Title VIII were to be spent for the training of skilled technicians in occupations necessary to the national defense. Funds were authorized for a four-year period. All monies were provided to the states on a dollar-for-dollar matching basis.

Title IV of the NDEA also had direct effect on college- and university-level occupational education programs. Monies were provided to over 1,000 graduate students in approximately 120 institutions of higher education during the first year of the Act to promote the training of college teachers through a fellowship program. Each fellow received a stipend of $2,000 the first year, $2,200 the second year, and $2,400 the third year, plus a $400-per-year-per-dependent stipend. Many college and university teachers in occupational education today were trained under this enactment.

Perhaps the most significant effects of this Act did not grow directly out of the funding of its various titles, but, rather, started or fanned the flames of a public interested in *all* students going to college. Through the passage of this Act, the U.S. government, in effect, told every American that he or she should attend a college or university. The effects of this attitude have, until recently, inhibited the development of programs other than baccalaureate degree occupational programs in this country. Many talented students have not entered occupational training programs because of the effects of the "go to college" syndrome. This occurred even in the face of extensive manpower data indicating a dire need for specific occupational training in areas needing less than baccalaureate-degree personnel and an excess in many areas requiring B.S.-level training.

The NDEA, while representing a partnership between vocational and nonvocational training, also represented and supported a national trend destined to prove extremely wasteful in manpower utilization and human-need fulfillment.

National Defense Education Act Extended 1961

Title VIII of the NDEA was extended by the 87th Congress under the Public Law 87-344. The Act was extended for two years and the area vocational center concept was to be expanded in the Vocational Education Act of 1963. Different titles of the NDEA were of course amended under several different enactments. Many of these amendments, while not necessarily related to vocational education, are alive and well in different enactments, and the effects of the NDEA of 1958 will be felt in decades to come in both vocational and nonvocational training.

Higher Education Facilities Act (HEFA) 1963

On December 16, 1963, the Higher Education Facilities Act (HEFA) was approved. This enactment authorized a five-year program of federal grants and loans to colleges and universities for the expansion and new development of physical facilities. As the Vanguard rockets continued to fail on their launching pads, the American public was made even more aware of a need for highly skilled technical competence. The great college and university enrollment increases brought about in part by the NDEA made the expansion of higher education physical facilities a must. As a result of this, Congress passed the HEFA.

Funds from this Act went to both public and private, nonprofit colleges and universities. The Commissioner of Education was the administering agent. The federal government matched state funds by a 40-percent (federal) to a 60-percent (state) ratio for public institutions. Private, nonprofit institutions received 33⅓-percent federal matching for facilities, provided basic guidelines were met.

Seventy-eight percent of allocated funds to the state was to be used for the construction of undergraduate academic facilities to be based on the enrollments in institutions of higher education and high schools. Twenty-two percent of allocated funds under Title I was to go to junior college facilities. This was based on the number of high school graduates in the state.

Title II of the HEFA provided funds for the construction of *graduate* academic facilities. Federal matching was not to exceed 33⅓ percent of the cost of construction of any approved project in the state. Appropriation for this title could not exceed 12½ percent of total state appropriation.

While Titles I and II were grants to states, Title III was for loans to states for the construction of both graduate and undergraduate facilities. Under this Title, no single state could borrow more than 12½ percent of its total authorized funds and not more than 75 percent of the total cost of an approved project could be borrowed.

The HEFA provided much-needed federal assistance to junior colleges, undergraduate programs, and graduate programs involved in training skilled technicians. Many occupational programs in various community colleges in the United States owe much of their physical housing to the Higher Education Facilities Act.

Elementary and Secondary Education Act (ESEA) 1965

As the space exploration programs began to meet with success, people began to question certain other facets of education in the United States. The technical competence was available to launch rockets into outerspace, but a very high degree of illiteracy existed in rural and urban areas of the country. The existence of poverty and cultural deprivation contrasted with the large amount of federal money spent on education. During the early 1960s, segregation became a national issue as it related to our nation's schools. Shrinking local resources resulting from a climbing rate of inflation limited the financial resources necessary to develop sound local school programs. An analysis of students entering the highly refined technical programs of the NDEA era indicated that early education programs needed improvement.

These factors plus many others led to the passage of two major legislative enactments in 1965. President Lyndon B. Johnson remarked upon signing the Higher Education Act of 1965 on November 8, of that year:

> I consider the Higher Education Act with its companion, the Elementary and Secondary Education Act of 1965, which we signed back in the Spring of this year, to be the keystones of the great . . . 89th Congress.

The Elementary and Secondary Education Act was specifically designed to provide sound educational opportunities to youngsters between the ages of five and seventeen. Particular emphasis was placed on the education of students from low-income families. The Act consisted of five Titles. An analysis of these titles follows.

Title I

The major purpose for Title I of the ESEA was to strengthen local education agencies and to provide additional assistance to areas serving low-income and educationally deprived youngsters. The largest percentage of all resources provided through this Act was in this Title.

Title II

Title II provided resources in the areas of school libraries, textbooks, and other instructional materials. This title established a five-year program for providing grants to states. Title II provided all manner of public and private schools with financial resources to purchase needed instructional supplies and equipment.

Title III

The major purpose of Title III of the ESEA was to provide financial assistance to agencies developing exemplary programs and projects that would serve as models for regular school programs. This type of provision also was to be found in vocational education legislation of that time, and it marks a major, perhaps philosophical, change in educational legislation.

In funding exemplary activities as models for regular school programs, Congress has left the "stuff" of education up to the professionals. That is, funds were made available for education program planning within the ranks of the professional educator. No longer does Congress dictate *specific* programs.

It is interesting to note, however, at the time of this writing, these very provisions found in contemporary education are coming under fire. The inference this writer draws from this is that some national leaders are questioning the competence of educational leadership in determining professional direction.

Title IV

Title IV of the ESEA provided resources to U.S. Office of Economic Opportunity (USOE) and state agencies for educational research and research training. Funds also were authorized for the construction of research facilities.

Title V

Financial support and assistance to State Departments of Education were assured through Title V of the Act. Major emphasis was on leadership development in State Offices of Education.

The ESEA was amended in 1967. Additional titles such as *Federally Affected Areas, Extension of Adult Education Program,* and *Bilingual Education Programs* were added. It was clear that major educational emphasis was not directed toward answering many social, educational, and economic problems at the local education agency level.

Higher Education Act 1965

As mentioned earlier, the Higher Education Act of 1965 and the Elementary and Secondary Education Act of 1965 were, in effect, companion enactments (not to be confused with "companion bills"). Both enactments, while their passage was more than six months apart, were based on a similar theme. That theme centered about the *local* agency and its needs to satisfy *local* educational problems.

The reason this theme evolved should be fairly clear. Previous legislation, such as the NDEA of 1958, placed major emphasis on central or national control for education. As a result, local problems grew and festered until rioting, unrest, and turmoil existed in nearly every community. It was clear that federal-level management and decision making could not alleviate local problems. Conversely, however, in problem areas such as segregation, it was also clear that in many cases, local agencies could not solve local problems. To date, many of these questions continue to go unsolved—take a look at busing!

As previously stated, the Higher Education Act was aimed at providing assistance to colleges and universities in the solution of local problems. In fact, Title I of the Act was called *Community Service and Continuing Education Programs*. Under this Title, states were authorized funds to conduct extension activities that would serve the needs of the community. This would be contingent upon the approval of a state plan. A National Advisory Council on Extension and Continuing Education was also established under this Title.

Title II of the Higher Education Act authorized funds to states to improve libraries of higher education agencies.

Title III of this Act was designed to help develop institutions through a system of grants.

Title IV provided financial assistance to needy students through a system of "educational opportunity grants" and a subsidized low-interest, insured-loan payment. This Title assured financial assistance to students who normally would not be able to afford to go to college.

Title V of the Higher Education Act, in order to assure highly qualified teaching personnel, established the National Teacher Corps. This Title of the Act later would become the well-known Educational Professions Development Act (EPDA) later passed in 1967.

Title VI authorized funds for special classroom materials.

Title VII amended the Higher Education Facilities Act.

Education Professions Development Act (EPDA) 1967

The Education Professions Development Act (EPDA) was considered by many of its proponents as a landmark in educational legislation. It was designed to be a cohesive force, joining together all teacher education elements of former legislation. In meeting this end, it was somewhat a failure. It lacked the flexibility to remain an omnibus enactment. Its various parts, sections, and subsections have undergone many amendments by more recent legislation, such as the Higher Education Amendments of that same year.

Despite this weakness, however, the EPDA, with all of its amendments and revisions, is alive and well at the time of this writing. Some of its provisions have been incorporated into the Education Amendments of 1972 (See chapter 6).

The EPDA was created when Title V of the Higher Education Act of 1965 was amended. EPDA broadened Title V to include five personnel-preparation programs. These were:

1. National Teacher Corps
2. Teachers in areas of critical shortage
3. Fellowships for teachers and other educational professionals
4. Improved opportunities for training for personnel serving in areas other than higher education
5. Training programs for higher education personnel, and upon passage of the Vocational Education Amendments of 1968, training for vocational education personnel

The EPDA consisted of six major parts. The provisions of each are as follows.

Part A

This part of the Act was designed to attract qualified persons to the field of education. Various agencies were to receive funds to encourage youth and adults to look at a future in education.

Part B-1

The National Teacher Corps was continued in areas with concentrations of low-income families. The goal of this program was improved educational opportunities for future teachers through improved teacher training programs.

Part B-2

This part of the Act was designed to meet critical teacher shortages in specific areas. Funds authorized and appropriated to state education agencies were designed to be used to attract people into teaching and to recruit teacher aides.

Part C

Monies were appropriated from this part of the Act for teacher and related-personnel fellowships in areas such as preschool, elementary school, vocational education, and others.

Part D

Part D monies were to be used for training and retraining activities for teachers and teacher trainers, supervisors and administrators, service personnel, and teacher aides.

Part E

Part E monies were to be used for training persons serving or preparing to serve as teachers, administrators, or educational specialists in higher education.

Summary

It might be said that the Sputnik era of educational legislation (at least, as it is defined here) has seen the greatest diversity in the theme and purpose of its enactments. Within only a decade, from 1958 to 1968, the total emphasis on education moved from highly skilled, centrally controlled, technical education programs to a culturally oriented, local-need type of program. Within that short decade, educational legislation was passed to correct problems that had arisen out of legislation passed only a few years earlier.

As students of educational legislation, we view that era as one of great change, as perhaps a time of many errors. However, in analyzing legislation of the late 1960s (EPDA in particular) and in looking at educational problem areas of the early 1970s, it is clear to see that in remedying errors through various enactments, new problems arise. Specifically, the EPDA was passed to help fill a need for educational professionals; yet, in 1972, a surplus of teachers existed.

Questions for Review

1. What, in your opinion, was the cause of the massive manpower shortages in the mathematics, science, and technical areas prior to the passage of the National Defense Education Act in 1958?

2. What caused the emphasis on area vocational centers and their enabling legislation under the NDEA?

3. Have any community colleges in your state received building assistance through the Higher Education Facilities Act?

4. Did State Departments of Education change their roles with respect to statewide management of secondary schools through the ESEA? If so, how? If not, why was this section included in the Act, and why did it fail?

5. What specific sections of the EPDA provide leadership training funds for people in state offices, etc.?

Suggested Activities

1. Prepare a written analysis of the specific effects the NDEA has had on the national manpower utilization since its passage.

2. Through review of old newspapers and magazines, list several events that made national headlines which may have led to the eventual enactment of the Elementary and Secondary Education Act.

3. List several exemplary programs within your state that received their initial funding through the ESEA.

4. Analyze the status that vocational education programs had with respect to the ESEA. Describe the effects, if any, that the Vocational Education Act of 1963 had on the ESEA.

5. Prepare a list of teacher education programs that are supported wholly or in part by EPDA funds.

Bibliography

Barlow, Melvin L. *History of Industrial Education in the United States.* Peoria, Ill.: Bennett, 1967.

Borrow. *Man in a World at Work.* Boston: Houghton Mifflin, 1964.

Burt, Samuel. *Industry and Vocational Technical Education.* McGraw-Hill, 1967.

Ellis, Harlan Reed. "EPDA—To Meet a Critical Need," *American Education* 33 (March 1969): 359.

Davies, Don. "Getting into EPD Act," *American Vocational Journal* 6 (September 1969).

Halperin, Samuel. "Education Legislation in the 90th Congress," *Phi Delta Kappan* 48, no. 6 (February 1967).

Harshorn, Mervill E. "EPDA Program Priorities for 1970," *Social Education* 33 (1969): 62.

Levitan, S. A. *Federal Manpower Politics and Programs to Combat Underemployment.* Michigan: W. E. Upjohn Institute for Employment Research, 1964.

Manpower Report of the President. Washington D.C.: Government Printing Office, 1963.

Roberts, Roy W. *Vocational and Practical Arts Education.* New York: Harper, 1965.

Swanson. *Development of Federal Legislation for Vocational Education.* Chicago: American Technical Society, 1962.

"Teacher-Training Programs Ready for EPDA Debuts," *School Shop* 28 (February 1969): 62.

"The Education Professions: A Report on the People Who Serve Our Schools and Colleges, 1968," U.S. Dept. of Health, Education, and Welfare, Office of Education, U.S. Printing Office, Washington, D.C.: 1969.

4

Getting at the Issues: *The VEA '63 and the '68 Amendments*

Objectives

- The student will conduct a thorough review of literature concerned with the Vocational Education Act of 1963.
- The student will describe the conceptual differences between these enactments and previous vocational education legislation.
- The student will describe the major contributions of these enactments to contemporary occupational education.

Introduction

Expanding un- and under-employment, racial unrest, social turmoil and other major factors began coming to light in the late 1950s and early 1960s. To most concerned vocational educators, it appeared that the traditional concept of providing vocational training to a limited number of students in a limited number of areas was not effective in a society requiring vast numbers of technically trained personnel. An increasing emphasis on job enlargement and women in the work force began to demonstrate that classic vocational education was indeed ready for change.

The designers of the Vocational Education Act of 1963 and its '68 Amendments were concerned with the "people" aspect of vocational education. "Programs for people," rather than "people for programs," became the central theme of this legislation. A thorough analysis of each of the aforementioned enactments follows.

37

The Vocational Education Act 1963

Legislation, in particular occupational education legislation, is a process through which a cultural need is identified, interpreted, and acted upon in relationship to the various pressing economic, political, professional, and social factors characteristic of the society at a specific point in time. It can be postulated, therefore, that the study of a society's legislative enactments is a study of the society itself. If one were to analyze all the occupational education legislation beginning with the Morrill Land Grant Act of 1862 and extending to the Vocational Education Amendments of 1968, one would note a progressive evolution and expansion of occupational education legislation to include new areas of study resulting from a rapid rate of change in technology. The purpose of this chapter is not to present a detailed description of legislative evolution, but rather to present an in-depth analysis of two legislative enactments: The Vocational Education Act of 1963 and The Vocational Education Amendments of 1968. However, one first must understand the events and circumstances resulting in these legislative Acts, to develop a common basis for interpreting the various provisions set forth in the Acts.

The early 1960s saw a dramatic rise in youth unemployment and underemployment: a tremendous personnel shortage in many technical, semiprofessional, and skilled occupations; an increase in the retraining and continuing education needs of workers displaced by automation; and a rising demand for new educational opportunities, both at the secondary and post-secondary levels. These pressing factors forced the people of the United States to reexamine their long-standing neglect of occupational education. President John F. Kennedy initiated the reappraisal on February 20, 1961, in his message to the Congress on American education. In this message, the late President said, ". . . technological changes which have occurred in all occupations call for a review and reevaluation of these Acts, with a view toward their modernization." The Acts President Kennedy referred to in his message are the National Vocational Education Acts, first enacted by the Congress of the United States in 1917 and subsequently amended. President Kennedy requested the Secretary of Health, Education, and Welfare to convene an advisory body drawn from educational professions, labor, industry, and agriculture as well as the lay public, to be responsible for reviewing and evaluating the current

National Vocational Education Acts and to make recommendations for improving and redirecting the vocational education program.

The Secretary of Health, Education and Welfare, A. J. Celebrezze, appointed Benjamin C. Willis, Chicago school superintendent, as chairman of the Panel of Consultants on Vocational Education. The Panel concluded its study in November, 1962, and published its findings in 1963 in a full report entitled, *Education for a Changing World of Work*. In this report, the Panel recommended that the fifty-seven-million-dollar federal appropriation to vocational education be increased to four hundred million dollars. Also, the Panel requested that the occupational categories specified by previous enactments be replaced by a more flexible organizational structure.

The Perkins-Morse Bill, better known as the Vocational Education Act of 1963 (Public Law 88-210) enacted into law on December 18, 1963, by President Lyndon B. Johnson, represented a compromise between two widely varying points of view. The traditional viewpoint contended that all new legislation should be designed along the lines of the Smith-Hughes Act, while the other viewpoint argued for the Smith-Hughes and George-Barden Acts in order to make a fresh start. Congress, in effect, amended the Smith-Hughes and the George-Barden Acts, but the various administrative agencies implemented, in many cases, entirely new programs of vocational education.

Within the framework of the Vocational Education Act of 1963, a new-type federal-state cooperative vocational education program was enacted into law. The central theme of this program is manifested by broadened conceptions of education for work and real emphasis on serving the youth of this country. The new program and the amendments to the Smith-Hughes and the George-Barden Acts functioned to remove the restrictiveness that had made these Acts increasingly outdated. The Declaration of Purpose, Section 1, emphasized the need for program flexibility in order to provide ". . . vocational training or retraining which is of high quality, which is realistic in the light of actual or anticipated opportunities for gainful employment, and which is suited to their needs, interests, and ability to benefit from such training." In this initial section, it is the intent of Congress to establish the central themes of program flexibility and adaptability based upon the concept of "programs for people" within a dynamic labor market.

Section 2 of the Act, which is the Authorization of Appropriations, authorized the following appropriations:

Fiscal year ending June 30, 1964............$ 60,000,000
Fiscal year ending June 30, 1965.............118,500,000
Fiscal year ending June 30, 1966.............177,500,000
Fiscal year ending June 30, 1967
    and each fiscal year thereafter 225,000,000

Unlike the allocation formula found in previous legislation, this Act declared that 90 percent of the sums appropriated was to be allotted on the basis of state's population with some provision for equalization based upon a per capita income allotment ratio.

A state, in accordance with its approved state plan, was able to use federal funds for any or all of the following purposes:

1. Vocational education for persons attending high school
2. Vocational education for persons who have completed or left high school and who are available for full-time study in preparation for entering the labor market
3. Vocational education for persons (other than persons who are receiving training allowances under the Manpower Development and Training Act of 1962, the Area Redevelopment Act, or the Trade Expansion Act of 1962) who have already entered the labor market and who need training or retraining to achieve stability or advancement in employment
4. Vocational education for persons who have academic, socio-economic, or other handicaps that prevent them from succeeding in the regular vocational education program
5. Construction of area vocational education school facilities
6. Ancillary services and activities to assure quality in all vocational education programs.

At least 25 percent of each state's allotment for each fiscal year was to be used for the purposes set forth in (2) or (5) listed above. Also, a state must reserve 3 percent of its fiscal allocation to be used only for the purposes set forth in (6) above. Ten percent of the sums appropriated for each fiscal year was to be used by the Commissioner of Education to allocate on a project-grant basis for specific research, teacher training, curriculum development, and experimental or demonstrative projects in vocational education.

A state desiring to receive its allotment of federal funds must submit through its state board (established by the Smith-Hughes Act) to the Commissioner of Education a state plan. This plan should describe in detail the provisions the state incorporated for the supervision and the administration of its vocational education programs. The plan must set forth the policies, the procedures, and the controls to be followed by the state in using federal funds. Approval of the plan by the Commissioner of Education was required before a state could receive its allocation.

The Vocational Education Act of 1963 established in the Office of Education, an Advisory Committee on Vocational Education. The Committee is composed of the Commissioner of Education, who acts as chair, one representative each of the Departments of Commerce, Agriculture, and Labor, and twelve members appointed by the Commissioner of Education with the approval of the Secretary of Health, Education, and Welfare. Of these twelve representatives of the general public, not more than six members could be professional educators. This Committee was established for the purpose of advising the Commissioner of Education on the national administration of the vocational education program in light of relating the program to actual training requirements. The Committee could not meet less than twice a year and was subject to call by the Commissioner of Education.

Within the framework of the Vocational Education Act of 1963, two major, highly influential Vocational Education Acts were amended. The amendments to the Smith-Hughes and the George-Barden Acts revolutionized and expanded the scope of education for work. For the first time in the history of vocational education legislation, states were allowed to transfer or combine categorical training allotments.

Congress, recognizing the need for continual program evaluation and upgrading, provided for a periodic review of vocational education programs and laws. This provision within the Vocational Education Act of 1963 required the Secretary of Health, Education, and Welfare to appoint an Advisory Council on Vocational Education during 1966 with the intent of reviewing the administration of the vocational education programs, and making recommendations for improvements of such administration. The Council was to be composed of twelve members familiar with the vocational needs of management and labor. A report of its findings and recommendations was to be submitted not later than January 1, 1968. The Secretary was further ordered to convene the Advisory Council from time to time at intervals of not more than five years. Since its initial report, *Vocational Education: A Bridge Between Man and His Work*, the Council has released four subsequent reports concerning the state of vocational education in the nation.

The Work-Study programs for vocational education students were enacted into law by the Vocational Education Act of 1963. This program simply allows a student who is in financial need to become employed in order to commence or continue his or her vocational education. The student must be at least fifteen years of age and less than twenty-one years of age at the commencement of employment. He or she must be enrolled in a vocational education program, remain in good standing, and be in full attendance. Compensations must not exceed forty-five dollars per month or three hundred fifty dollars per academic year.

The Vocational Education Act of 1963, like its forerunner the Smith-Hughes Act, represented a mighty landmark case for vocational education legislation—an important landmark, since it represented a new philosophy in the relationship between education and work in the United States. During the implementation of the Vocational Education Act of 1963, vocational education was faced with the realities of, and the problems caused by, the existing structure of vocational education. The structure, which was a product of many conflicting educational-training movements and several acute periods of manpower shortages, allowed only for a narrow range of education for work. From this rigid system of vocational education, Congress attempted to legislate a program which would be flexible and adaptive enough to meet the diversified needs of a growing nation and its people and, at the same time, be efficiently administered at all governing levels.

The Vocational Education Amendments 1968

It was Congressman Roman Pucinski and Senator Wayne Morse who pushed for the passing of Public Law 90-576, better known as the Vocational Education Amendments of 1968. This bill moved through Congress at a time when Washington was increasing taxes, cutting the budget, responding to the increased seriousness of the Viet Nam conflict, and working to extend the Higher Education Act. However, the importance of vocational education was seen and the bill was signed into law by President Johnson on October 16, 1968.

The Vocational Education Amendments of 1968 can be functionally broken down into 11 parts (Title I A-I, Title II part F, and Title III). The first section deals with the Acts General Provisions; it declared the same purpose as the '63 Act, but emphasized vocational education in post-secondary schools. The definition of vocational education also was broadened to bring it closer to general education. Provisions were made for a 21-member National Advisory Council to be appointed by the President of the United States.

Part B of the Act dealt with the uses of federal funds for State Vocational Education programs. The uses of these funds remained basically the same as in the '63 Act, except for the addition of funds for programs for handicapped persons, vocational guidance and counseling, and private vocational training institutions. Federal funding also is available to states with the approval of its State Plan by the Commissioner of Education.

Part C of the new Amendments was of great importance because it rewrote Section 4 (c) of the '63 Act, which provided federal funds for state-based research. This rewritten section provided greater control through increased financial resources for vocational education research and curriculum development at the national level. This was to provide much closer coordination among federally funded research and development projects.

Part D of the Amendments earmarked funds for new exemplary programs and projects; the funding for these programs was aimed at bringing about new ways to bridge the gap between school and work. These programs are not only for young people still in school but also for those who have dropped out or graduated. Specifically, it earmarked funds for:

1. Those programs or projects designed to familiarize elementary and secondary school students with the broad range of occupations for which special skills are required and the requisites for careers in such occupations
2. Programs or projects for students providing educational experiences through work during the school year or in the summer

3. Programs or projects for intensive occupational guidance and counseling during the last years of school and for initial job placement
4. Programs or projects designed to broaden or improve vocational education curriculums
5. Exchanges of personnel between schools and other agencies, institutions, or organizations participating in activities to achieve the purposes of this part, including manpower agencies and industry
6. Programs or projects for young workers released from their jobs on a part-time basis for the purpose of increasing their educational attainment
7. Programs and projects at the secondary level to motivate and provide preprofessional preparation for potential teachers for vocational education

A three-year limit to the financing of these types of programs or projects is included.

Residential vocational education, as set forth in Part E of the Vocational Education Amendments of 1968, was virtually the same as set forth in the '63 Act. Once again, the residential school concept did not grow to fruition.

Consumer and Homemaking Education, Part F, was not a program which was pointed solely at employment for young people, but rather was concerned with preparing people for the work role of homemaker. There were two major purposes for this Part of the Amendments. Money was authorized for educational programs that: (1) provide home economics aimed at the cultural and social conditions of economically depressed areas; (2) encourage leadership preparation; (3) prepare youth and adults in the dual role of homemaker and wage earner; and (4) maintain adequate "ancillary services, activities, and other means of assuring quality in all homemaking education programs . . ." This section of the Act was aimed at helping disadvantaged people to cope with and survive in their environment.

Another new program with earmarked funds was the Cooperative Education Programs (Part G). Cooperative vocational education programs were specifically provided for with earmarked funds to cover the costs of coordination and instruction, reimbursement of employers for certain expenses, and student costs, including transportation. In order that a state may be funded under the provisions of this program, their plan had to assure the following:

1. Funds from this section must be used only for cooperative programs.
2. Cooperative efforts with such agencies as labor groups, employment agencies, employers, and community agencies should be the basis of program development.
3. Provisions must be made for reimbursement of added costs to employers for on-the-job training of students enrolled in cooperative programs.
4. Program quality must be assured through ancillary services and activities.
5. Priority of funding cooperative programs must be given to areas that have high rates of school dropouts and youth unemployment.

The cooperative program has taken on great importance in the training of young people. It not only helps teach the young person to cope with the real world and gain work experience, but when combined with the work study program (Part H), the student also can earn a small income, which could make staying in school much more likely. To qualify for work study programs a student must: (1) be a full-time student in a vocational program; (2) need an income to start or to continue vocational training; (3) be between 15 and 21 years of age; and (4) work no longer than 15 hours a week for $45 per month or $350 per academic year.

Part I of the 1968 Amendments earmarked funds for curriculum development. This Part of the Act also repealed many vocational education acts enacted prior to the signing of the Vocational Education Amendments of 1968.

Title III of the 1968 Amendments is actually an amendment to the Higher Education Act of 1965. This section was titled, "Vocational Education Leadership and Professional Development." Through Part F of this Act (Higher Education Act of 1965), vocational education leadership and professional development are provided funds for training and development programs, institutes, and in-service education for vocational education teachers, supervisors, coordinators, and administrators; advanced study for experienced vocational educators; exchange of personnel; and leadership awards, stipends, allowances, and other expenses.

The last section of the 1968 Amendments (Title III) was titled, "Miscellaneous Provisions." Among several miscellaneous provisions, the Commissioner was directed to study how the Job Corps, under the economic opportunity program, might be transferred to the federal-state vocational education program. In addition, certain amendments were made in the area of adult education, elementary and secondary education, and educational professional development.

Summary

The Vocational Education Act of 1963 and the Vocational Education Amendments of 1968 have done much to help vocational education programs develop into viable systems designed to meet various societal and personal needs. Both the '63 Act and the '68 Amendments represented a major change of thought regarding vocational education. Most professionals and concerned lay citizens viewed these enactments as clear mandates to vocational education personnel to develop programs to meet the specific occupational needs of the individual and the country.

Questions for Review

1. What were some of the major factors that led to the passage of the Vocational Education Act of 1963?

2. What group of individuals was most instrumental in determining the content and purpose of the Vocational Education Amendments of 1968?

3. What is the importance of the new Part C—Research and Training in Vocational Education found in the 1968 Vocational Education Amendments?

4. What major social factors may have led to the passage of the 1968 Amendments?

5. What are some of the major conceptual differences between the 1963 Act and its 1968 Amendments and the vocational education legislation that preceded their passage?

Suggested Activities

1. Develop a comparison chart that compares and contrasts the major parts of the Smith-Hughes, VEA '63, and the '68 Amendments. After the chart is complete, analyze each major area of difference and discuss the reasons for the variations.

2. Obtain a copy of your local State Plan. Compare the major State Plan provisions with the major sections of the '68 Amendments.

3. Obtain a copy of a local education agency plan. Determine whether or not it parallels the State Plan.

4. Develop a plan for a Residential Vocational School. Propose such things as geographic locations within the state, types of people to be served, programs to be offered, and administrative structure. Does this give you any indication as to why residential vocational schools were not funded? Compare the residential school plan with Job Corps.

5. Contact your State Office of Vocational Education and request a description of the programs and projects funded under Part D—Exemplary Programs and Projects of the '68 Amendments.

Bibliography

A State Plan of the Administration of Vocational and Technical Education in Illinois, Board of Vocational Education and Rehabilitation, State of Illinois, December 1970.

Arnold, Walter. "Changing Patterns in Vocational Education." *Industrial Arts and Vocational Education,* December 1964, 206.

———"Washington Report." *Industrial Arts and Vocational Education,* May 1968, 1; September 1968, 1; November 1968, 1; and December 1968, 1.

Barlow, Melvin L. *History of Industrial Education in the United States.* Peoria, Ill.: Bennett, 1967.

Beaumont, J. A. "Broadened Scope of Vocational Education." *American Vocational Journal* 44:19 and April 1969.

Borrow. *Man in a World at Work.* Boston: Houghton Mifflin, 1964.

Burt, Samuel. *Industry and Vocational Technical Education.* McGraw-Hill, 1967.

Dick, A. A. "Master Plan for Vocational Education." *Industrial Arts and Vocational Education* 58 (March 1969): 70.

Evans, R. N., Mangum, G. L., and Pragan, O. *Education For Employment; The Background and Potential of the 1968 Vocational Educational Amendments.* Ann Arbor, Mich.: The Institute of Industrial Relations, 1969.

"Federal Role in Education." *Congressional Quarterly Service.* R 379.12 C749f, 1969.

Guy, Hollis. "Public Law 88-210, Part A-Vocational Education." *Business Education Forum* 18 (January 1964): 25.

Levitan, S. A. *Federal Manpower Policies and Programs to Combat Underemployment.* Kalamazoo, Mich.: W. E. Upjohn Institute for Employment Research, 1964.

———and Mangum, G. L. *Federal Training and Work Programs in the Sixties,* Ann Arbor, Mich.: Institute of Labor and Industrial Relations, 1969.

Manpower Report of the President. Washington, D. C.: U.S. Government Printing Office, 1963.

Prakken, Lawrence. "Congressional Agreement Reached on Perkins Bill as AVA Meets for 57th Annual Convention," *School Shop* 23 (February 1964): 47.

Public Law 88-210, Vocational Education Act of 1963.

Public Law 90-576, Vocational Education Amendments of 1968.

Roberts, Roy W. *Vocational and Practical Arts Education.* 2nd ed. New York: Harper, 1965.

———3rd ed. 1971.

Schuchat, Theodore. "The Vocational Education Act of 1963: What's in it for you," *School Shop* 23 (April 1964): 30.

Tonne, Herbert A. "The Vocational Education Act of 1963 and Suggested Lines of Action," *Business Education Forum* 18 (February 1964): 29.

U. S. Office of Education. "The Vocational Education Act," *School Life* 46 (March-April 1964): 3.

———*"Vocational Education: The Bridge between Man and His Work,"* Washington, D.C.: U. S. Government Printing Office, November 1968.

———*"Reports on the Implementation of the Vocational Education Amendments of 1968,"* Washington, D. C.: U. S. Government Printing Office, November 1971.

Venn, Grant; *Man, Education and Work*. Washington D.C.: U. S. Government Printing Office, 1964.

Notes and Revisions

The Department of Labor: *Training and Retraining for the Job Market*

Objectives

- The student will review information concerned with the various Department of Labor or Manpower legislative enactments.
- The student will describe the conceptual differences between the Department of Labor approach to vocational training and the vocational education programs commonly administered by the Office of Education.
- The student will analyze political and economic decisions that have affected Manpower programs.
- The student will describe the effects that Manpower legislation has had on current occupational and career education programs and clientele.

Introduction

Over the years, occupational education has been divided and categorized in many ways. One of the more common ways was to divide occupational programs into two categories; one is concerned with initial vocational training, and one is concerned with vocational retraining for specific job markets. Traditionally, many of the Manpower or Department of Labor programs have been aimed at retraining underemployed or unemployed adults. Programs such as Job Corps, etc., were, however, also aimed at initial training for target groups.

The specific effects of the Department of Labor type of manpower programs have not been felt. It will, therefore, be advantageous to analyze Department of Labor programs that have been implemented through various legislative enactments. Also included in this chapter is a brief analysis of a proposed enactment that was vetoed in December 1970. This bill is important, now, in itself, but is also an indicator of a general trend toward a lack of enthusiasm on the part of the administration and some members of Congress, as well as professionals, with regard to manpower types of programs.

Area Redevelopment Act 1961

The passage of the Area Redevelopment Act of 1961 represented an increasing awareness on the part of the federal government with regard to the economic deprivation of specific areas of the United States. This enactment provided several titles to assist individuals from these economically depressed areas to increase their employability.

An annual appropriation of $4.5 million was made to support vocational training under the Act. An additional sum of money was appropriated for subsistence payments to trainees.

Manpower Development and Training Act (MDTA) 1962

On March 15, 1962, Congress approved the MDTA. The Act authorized for appropriation in excess of $370 million over a period of three years.

The major purpose of the Act was to provide training opportunities for under- and unemployed individuals. This training was based on employment needs, as ascertained by the Department of Labor and local employment agencies.

The various vocational training programs were administered through existing state agencies for vocational education, as established by the Smith-Hughes and George-Barden Acts.

Economic Opportunity Act 1964

Public Law 88-452, the Economic Opportunity Act, was enacted on August 20, 1964. The law was established to strengthen and supplement existing legislation aimed at increasing the opportunities for everyone to receive education and training for work and to live in decency and dignity.

Several aspects of the Economic Opportunity Act (EOA) were quite significant with respect to vocational education. They were:

1. *Job Corps.* The purpose for the establishment of the Job Corps was to help young men and women between the ages of sixteen through twenty-one prepare for the responsibilities of citizenship and to increase their employability through residential training centers.

2. *Work-Training Programs.* Part B of the EOA provided for useful work experiences for young people between the ages of sixteen through twenty-one in public service and other types of State and local work-study programs. These programs were to be offered by public agencies or private nonprofit organizations at the State and local levels.

3. *Work-Study Programs.* Part C of the EOA was aimed at students from low-income families who were enrolled in institutions of higher education. Part-time employment was to be provided to these youngsters, which would enable them to continue their education.

4. *Work-Experience Programs.* Title V, Work-Experience Programs, was to provide and/or expand opportunities for work experience and other types of training to individuals who needed same, but were unable to support or care for themselves or their families.

Employment and Manpower Act

On December 16, 1970, President Nixon vetoed the Employment and Manpower Act. This was a comprehensive approach to funding and extending new and existing Manpower Programs. This veto marked the beginning of a general trend toward a lack of success for omnibus Manpower enactments.

In general, the veto message indicated that proposed manpower programs were ineffective in meeting the employment needs of target groups. In fact, it was noted that as much as 44 percent of the total proposed funding would go to "dead-end jobs in the public sector."

The importance of this proposed, yet unsuccessful, enactment is in the trend it began. That is, a move away from comprehensive manpower programs.

Comprehensive Employment and Training Act of 1973

With the enactment of the Manpower Development and Training Act (MDTA) of 1962 and the Economic Opportunity Act of 1964, the federal government became heavily involved in manpower training. Appropriation under these two laws alone supported more than a dozen training programs.

With many programs trying to meet the needs of the unemployed and the underemployed, there was considerable duplication of effort. Each bureaucratic layer of responsibility tended to decrease the efficiency, and ultimately, the effectiveness of the programs designed to alleviate the above-mentioned problems. To alleviate the problems of duplication of training programs and the multiple layers of bureaucratic responsibility, the Comprehensive Employment and Training Act was passed and became effective December 28, 1973.

President Nixon signed into law the Comprehensive Employment and Training Act of 1973. This legislation was the culmination of almost five years of manpower reform efforts by the Congress and the administration. The purpose of the new law was to decentralize and streamline the federal manpower training programs, to make them more administratively efficient, and to make them more responsive to the local employment and manpower needs. In an attempt to remove the bureaucratic problems associated with the former manpower programs, primary administration of the programs became the responsibility of "prime sponsors." Governments eligible to be prime sponsors are states, units of general local government with a population of 100,000 or more, certain combinations of local governments and—in exceptional circumstances—other combinations or units of local government. A state may be a prime sponsor in all areas not covered by local prime sponsors.

Under the new law, the numerous categorical programs previously authorized were, to a great extent, eliminated. Rather than operate separate projects, each state and local prime sponsor was to receive block grants. The prime sponsors were, in turn, required to plan and operate the manpower programs to meet local needs.

The grants were authorized by the Secretary of Labor, who also had the responsibility to assure that the prime sponsors complied with the provisions of the law.

The Comprehensive Employment and Training Act consisted of six titles: (1) Title I Comprehensive Manpower Service (2) Title II Public Employment Programs (3) Title III Special Federal Responsibilities (4) Title IV Job Corps (5) Title V National Commission for Manpower Policy, and (6) Title VI General Provisions.

The Act authorized appropriation of such funds as were necessary for carrying out the provisions of the Act. Specific provision was made to provide $250 million in 1974 and $350 million in 1975 of any amount appropriated for public service employment in areas of substantial unemployment.

The impact of this Act must be evaluated by each individual and at the local or state levels. Most agree that CETA has had some effect on vocational education programs. For prime sponsors have, in many cases, turned to the vocational schools to provide the necessary service and training programs.

Comprehensive Employment and Training Act Amendments of 1978: Public Law 95-524

The 1978 amendments to the Comprehensive Employment and Training Act represent a major overhaul of previous legislation. In the Statement of Purpose (P. L. 95-524, Sec. 2, 1978) Congress stated: ". . . it is further, the purpose of this Act to provide for the maximum feasible coordination of plans, programs, and activities under this Act with economic development, community development, and related activities such as vocational education, vocational rehabilitation, public assistance, self-employment training, and social service programs."

This statement of purpose reflects a genuine concern on the part of Congress for elimination of waste and duplication of effort. Much like the previously enacted legislation dealing specifically with vocational education, Congress has mandated that a system for evaluation and review be developed.

The basic administrative structure, involving prime sponsors, etc. remains the same. However, greater emphasis has been placed upon utilization of services and facilities which are currently available, with or without reimbursement from federal, state and local agencies, if they are deemed appropriate. Such services would include state employment services, state and local vocational schools, as well as the services of the state vocational rehabilitation agencies. These are but a few examples of agencies which could be utilized in developing a plan for employment and training. In fact, the act specifically states ". . . nothing contained herein shall be construed to limit the utilization of services and facilities of private agencies, institutions, and organizations which can, at comparable costs, provide substantially equivalent training or services."

Greater emphasis has been placed upon the utilization of public vocational education facilities and it is stressed that local plans should provide evidence of consultation with local or regional vocational education agencies that include local advisory councils established under section 105(a) of the Vocational Education Act of 1963. The prime sponsors planning council must include a representative of vocational education agencies.

States that desire to receive assistance under the provisions of this Act must also establish a state employment and training council. Representatives of the service deliverers ". . . shall include at least one representative of the State Board of Vocational Education and the Public Employment Service and one representative of the State Advisory Council on Vocational Education."

It is quite apparent that Congress intended that CETA prime sponsors and state and local vocational education agencies coordinate their efforts in providing occupational programs for the group of people served by this Act.

The Comprehensive Employment and Training Act Amendments of 1978 consist of eight titles: Title I Administrative Provisions; Title II Comprehensive Employment and Training Services; Title III Special Federal responsibilities; Title IV Youth Programs; Title V National Commission for Employment Policy; Title VI Counter-cyclical Public Service Employment Program; Title VII Private Sector Opportunities for the Economically Disadvantaged; Title VIII Young Adult Conservation Corps.

All of the regulations which apply to this legislation have not been finalized at this time. Several areas of concern have been identified. The

Department of Labor is serious about reducing the volume of regulations and beefing-up fraud and abuse prevention standards which are major components of P. L. 95-524. Monitoring fraud and abuse will be an on-going duty. A prime sponsor must establish and include a regular monitoring unit and procedure in its annual master plan. The monitoring unit must document its activities on a quarterly basis. The monitoring unit must also make sure participants are in fact eligible.

Part II Section 204 (a)(2) is of particular significance to vocational educators. This section requires that vocational education boards and prime sponsors, prior to entering any agreement, consult with other agencies involved in formulating the five-year plan for vocational education. This would include agencies such as vocational rehabilitation, Bureau of Education for the Handicapped, and others mentioned in the Act itself.

Title IV provides authorization for youth employment programs, such as demonstration programs, youth incentive projects, and youth community conservation and improvement.

Title VII has perhaps received the most attention from state and local governmental agencies. The purpose of this title is to provide for temporary employment during periods of high unemployment. It is the intent of Congress that employment be provided during periods when the national rate of unemployment is in excess of 4 percent, and the number of jobs funded shall be sufficient to provide jobs for 20 percent of the number of unemployed in excess of 4 percent.

The impact of this piece of legislation upon vocational programs has yet to be assessed. However, as the regulations are written and local plans for implementation are developed, each vocational educator will become involved in some manner with the training programs outlined under this legislation. State and local administrators must establish the linkage necessary for ensuring their participation in the development of these plans.

Summary

New CETA legislation has been written by Congress. As Congress considered this legislation, it was apparent that state and local vocational educators were to have a bigger stake in CETA programs. Furthermore, there is considerable concern that all CETA programs have an educational component; thus many public service or municipally made work projects must provide for considerable amounts of education along with the on-the-job activities.

The major question which must be asked is whether these programs accomplished what they intended to do. This question, and others like it, can be answered only after long-term human resource supply and demand studies are conducted.

Questions for Review

1. What social and political factors brought about the passage of the early Department of Labor, Manpower legislation?

2. In your opinion, why were MDTA programs administered through the state vocational education agencies, rather than through state employment bureaus?

3. How successful has Job Corps been? Why?

4. Why have recent major manpower legislative attempts been thwarted?

5. Do you think that manpower enactments aimed at specific target occupations (such as health occupations) will appear more or less frequently than in the past? Why?

6. What was the major intent of CETA legislation, and how did it affect the operation and control at the local level?

7. Do you feel that the increased flexibility for determining program needs at the local level has resulted in better programs and more trained people for the work force?

8. What has been one of the major criticisms of the public employment title of the CETA bill?

Suggested Activities

1. Develop a listing of occupations in which critical shortages exist. Identify whether or not these shortages are on a local, regional, or national basis. What does this tell you about manpower supply and demand models?

2. Develop a legislative blueprint outlining a proposed statewide manpower development program that would include:

a. A system of supply analysis
b. A system for interpreting demand
c. Target groups
d. A procedure for regional sensitivity
e. A built-in system of evaluation

3. Prepare a listing of occupations for which there is a major emphasis on training personnel. Is there a possibility of over-supply within the next few years? What can be done?

Bibliography

Barlow, Melvin L. *History of Industrial Education in the United States*. Peoria, Ill.: Bennett, 1967.

Beaumont, J. A. "Broadened Scope of Vocational Education," *American Vocational Journal* 44:19 and April 1969.

Borrow. *Man in a World at Work*. Boston: Houghton Mifflin, 1964.

Burt, Samuel, *Industry and Vocational Technical Education*. Mc-Graw-Hill, 1967.

Evans, R. N., Mangum, G. L., and Pragan, O. *Education For Employment; The Background and Potential of the 1968 Vocational Educational Amendments*. Ann Arbor, Mich.: The Institute of Industrial Relations, 1969.

"Federal Role in Education," *Congressional Quarterly Service*. R 379. 12 C749f, 1969.

Levitan, S. A. *Federal Manpower Policies and Programs to Combat Underemployment*. Kalamazoo, Michigan: W. E. Upjohn Institute for Employment Research, 1964.

P. L. 87 - 27, Area Redevelopment Act.

P. L. 87 - 416, Manpower Development and Training Act of 1962.

P. L. 88 - 210, Vocational Education Act of 1963.

P. L. 88 - 352, Civil Rights Act of 1964.

P. L. 88 - 452, Economic Opportunity Act.

P. L. 93 - 203, Comprehensive Employment and Training Act of 1973.

P. L. 95 - 524, Comprehensive Employment and Training Act Amendments of 1978.

6

The Education Amendments of 1972 and 1974: *Consolidated Educational Legislation*

Objectives

• The student will identify the changes in amendments of 1974 and explain the possible social factors which brought them about.

Introduction

The Education Amendments of 1972 and the subsequent amendments of 1974 represent the continued effort on the part of Congress to bring about consolidation of the previously enacted legislation. The eventual passage of the omnibus bill in 1972 came as no surprise to most educators. The subsequent amendments of 1974 also represent a continued effort to refine and consolidate educational programs. The Education Professions Development Act (EPDA) was an early attempt at such an enactment and it was passed five years before the Education Amendments of 1972. Vocational education personnel were particularly interested in the fate of these bills since only two years before, the Employment and Manpower Training Act had gone down to the presidential veto. This veto provided the impetus for the new Comprehensive Employment and Training Act (CETA) of 1973 which brought about the consolidation of the numerous manpower training projects funded by the United States Department of Labor. The specifics of this act were discussed previously in Chapter 5.

A thorough review of this legislation will reveal the fact that the executive branch of government and Congress were concerned about expanding the activity of federal agencies in local school and training projects.

Public Law 92-318 (Education Amendments of 1972) was an exciting authorization, although little progress had been made regarding appropriation for vocational or occupational education under its various titles. The Education Amendments of 1974 (Public Law 93-380) provided some significant priority areas for vocational education.

The Education Amendments of 1972 amended the Higher Education Act of 1965, the Vocational Education Act of 1963, the General Education Provisions Act, and the Elementary and Secondary Education Act of 1965. The Education Amendments of 1974 were enacted to extend and amend the Elementary and Secondary Education Act of 1965. Since these enactments have been discussed previously, the remainder of this chapter will be devoted to the new concepts or priority areas of the 1972 and 1974 Education Amendments which are of specific concern to vocational or occupational education.

Community Colleges and Occupational Education

Title X of the Education Amendments of 1972 was directed toward a new program of funding to community colleges in the various states and toward the expansion of occupational education offerings at the postsecondary and adult levels. The law required that any state wishing to receive assistance for the development of postsecondary programs must establish a state commission responsible for statewide planning for the expansion or improvement of postsecondary education programs in community colleges. This commission was known as the "1202 Commission." The 1202 Commissions in each of the states were to be "broadly and equitably representative of the general public and public and private nonprofit and proprietary institutions of postsecondary education in the state, including community colleges (as defined in Title X), junior colleges, postsecondary vocational schools, area vocational schools, technical institutes, and four-year institutions of higher education and branches thereof." It is interesting to note that much emphasis was placed on the vocational- or occupational education-related personnel from the local communities insofar as the makeup of the 1202 Commission was concerned. Part A of Title X is specifically aimed at the establishment and expansion of community college programs. The State Commissions must submit a statewide plan for the expansion and improvement of their educational programs in community colleges. The plan must: (1) designate areas of a state which do not have state-paid, low-tuition, or two-year colleges within a reasonable distance for students; (2) establish, expand, and improve community colleges to make the opportunity to attend available to all residents; (3) establish federal and nonfederal funding priorities to achieve the goal of availability; (4) recommend adequate state and local support in funding priorities; (5) find duplication in post-secondary programs and recommend elimination of same; and (6) develop a plan to achieve the goal, utilizing state-modified plans for federally assisted vocational education, community services, and academic facilities. Authorizations for this section are $50 million for fiscal year 1973, $75 million for fiscal year 1974, and $150 million for fiscal year 1975.

Part B of Title X of the education amendments of 1972 is entitled, "Occupational Education Programs." Part B was a result of a House of Representatives amendment to the Act. It was, in fact a proposed enactment of its own entitled *The Occupational Education Act of 1971*. It appears as Part B of Title X of Public Law 92-318 in a modified form. Once again, utilizing the state commissions established under Section 1202 of the Act, this part requires a comprehensive program of planning for the establishment and operation of occupational education programs. Authorizations for this part are: for fiscal year 1973, $100 million; for fiscal year 1974, $250 million; and for fiscal year 1975, $500 million. This part of the Act also would establish a Bureau of Occupational and Adult Education at the federal level which is responsible for all adult vocational and occupational education and manpower training programs within the Office of Education.

Vocational Education

Title II of the 1972 Education Amendments amended certain parts of the Vocational Education Act of 1963. The VEA of 1963 also was amended to clarify the definition of vocational education with respect to industrial arts programs and programs for training volunteer firemen.

Title II extended the Vocational Education Act of 1963 through fiscal year 1975. Sections dealing with exemplary programs and projects, residential vocational schools, consumer homemaking education, cooperative vocational education, and, of course, the National Advisory Council on Vocational Education were continued. Special emphasis was given to vocational education programs for the disadvantaged. The funding of these programs is as follows:

Sec. 102 (b)	Special Programs for the Disadvantaged	$40 million each year
Part D	Exemplary Programs and Projects	$75 million each year
Part E	Residential Vocational Schools	$35 million each model
	(programs [demonstration schools]; $15 million for state grants, and $5 million for interest grants each year)	
Part F	Consumer and Homemaking Education	$50 million each year
Part H	Work-Study Programs	$35 million each year
Part I	Curriculum Development	$10 million each year
	National Advisory Council on Vocational Education	$150 thousand each year

The National Institute of Education

Probably one of the most exciting sections of the Education Amendments of 1972 for many educators was Section 405 under Part A of Title III. This section set up the National Institute of Education (NIE) and authorized for appropriation a total of $550 million for grants to carry out the various research functions of the Institute without any fiscal year limitations.

The basis for the establishment for the National Institute of Education (NIE) was that high-quality education still was not available to each and every American, regardless of his race, color, religion, sex, national origin, or social class. In order to insure that this equality would exist, a much more dependable knowledge about the process of education needed to be discovered and Congress believed that only through sound research procedures could this understanding of the teaching-learning process really be understood.

In years past, this particular section of the Act may not have evoked as much interest on the part of vocational education personnel as it did at the time of the passage of the Act. The first request for proposal (RFP) came out of the National Institute of Education. These RFPs are primarily aimed at research regarding career development and career education. This area has been of utmost concern to vocational education personnel for the past several years.

The Education Amendments of 1974, Public Law 93-380

From a political point of view, 1974 will long be remembered as a year of tremendous change in the United States. In spite of the problems confronting Congress and the President, the Elementary and Secondary Education Act of 1965 was amended. These amendments are of particular interest to vocational and occupational educators in several specific areas: (1) The law encourages the development of a written individualized educational plan for each child participating in the ESEA Title I program. Title I is that part of the act which provides for special education programs and projects for educationally deprived children, or as is commonly known, students with special needs. (2) The second significant area is the Women's Educational Equality Act of 1974. This act seeks to bring about change in the number and types of educational programs available to women. (3) Career Education. This section establishes an Office of Career Education with a mandate to assist in the establishment of career education programs in the nation's schools. (4) Bilingual vocational training is recognized as an acute problem involving millions of citizens. If these individuals are to profit from vocational training, it must be provided in such a manner that the student can understand the teachings.

With a piece of legislation so complex and so broad in scope as the Education Amendments of 1974, a detailed description of it would be impossible in this text. Therefore highlights of the above-mentioned areas will be discussed because they appear to have the greatest significance for occupational education professional personnel.

Individualized Educational Plan (IEP)

Title I of the new law states that "it is the intent of the Congress to encourage where feasible the development for each educationally deprived child participating in a program under this Title of an individualized written educational plan (maintained and periodically evaluated), agreed upon jointly by the local education agency, a parent or guardian of the child, and, where appropriate, the child."

The above-mentioned section of the law is significant in that the vocational education teacher must now be involved in the development of the individualized educational plan if the educationally deprived student is to participate in his or her vocational program. Prior to the enactment of this legislation, the planning of the educational program for each child was largely the responsibility of the special education professionals within the state and local education agency. This legislation encourages full participation by all parties: parents, teachers, and school administration personnel. As a result, better linkages have been developed between special and vocational educators. There is also a greater concern on the part of both groups to provide a vocational program appropriate for each individual's needs.

Women's Educational Equality Act of 1974

Title IV of this law deals with two specific concerns which have been identified. Women's educational equity and career education are of immediate concern.

Congress found that educational programs in the United States are inequitable, as such programs relate to women, and frequently limit full participation of all individuals in American society.

Under this act the Commissioner was authorized to make grants and enter into contracts for the following activities:

1. The development, evaluation, and dissemination by the applicant of curricula, textbooks, and other educational materials related to educational equity

2. Preservice and inservice training for educational personnel, including guidance and counseling, with special emphasis on programs and activities designed to provide educational equity
3. Research, development, and educational activities designed to advance educational equity
4. Guidance and counseling activities, including the development of nondiscriminatory tests, designed to assure educational equity
5. Educational activities to increase opportunities for adult women, including continuing educational activities and programs for underemployed and unemployed women
6. The expansion and improvement of educational programs and activities for women in vocational education, career education, physical education, and educational administration.

The inclusion of this act in this legislation provided the incentive necessary for each state to develop programs in order to carry out the intent of the act. In addition to the grants and contracts authorized, the commissioner was authorized to carry out a program of small grants not to exceed $15,000.00 each to support innovative approaches to bringing about educational equity for women.

Career Education

A second major area under Title IV of the 1974 education amendments is section 406 which deals with career education. Congress has determined that:

1. Every child should be prepared for gainful or maximum employment and for full participation in society by the time he or she completes secondary education.
2. Each local educational agency (LEA) is obligated to prepare all children including the disadvantaged and handicapped child within the school district of such agency.
3. Each state and LEA should provide a career education program with a wide variety of career education options designed to maximize the student's employment and career possibilities.

In order to carry out the provisions of this section an Office of Career Education was established within the U.S. Office of Education. The Officer of Career Education is headed by a director who in turn reports directly to the United States Commissioner of Education.

Career education, as defined in the law, means an educational process designed:

1. To increase the relationship between schools and society as a whole

2. To provide opportunities for counseling, guidance, and career development for all children

3. To relate the subject matter of the curricula of schools to the needs of persons to function in society

4. To extend the concept of the education progress beyond the school into the area of employment and the community

5. To foster flexibility in attitudes, skills, and knowledge in order to enable persons to cope with accelerating change and obsolescence

6. To make education more relevant to employment and to the need to function in society

7. To eliminate any distinction between education for vocational purposes and general or academic education.

This section of the law required the commissioner to conduct an assessment of the state of the art at the time of the enactment. It also provided for the establishment of an advisory committee which in turn would make recommendations for new legislation, designed to implement the goals of career education as outlined by the law.

As has been the case with other educational legislation, this section also allows the commissioner to make grants to state and local educational agencies, to develop and demonstrate projects in order to determine the most effective methods of introducing career education concepts into the school curriculum. In order to carry out the provisions of this act, the commissioner was authorized to expend up to $15,000,000 each fiscal year prior to 1 July 1978. The actual appropriation by Congress has been around $10,000,000 for each fiscal year.

The career education concept and movement has been an important factor in education for many years prior to the education amendments of 1974. However, at this point in time, Congress recognized the importance and provided separate funding for career education. Prior to this act, a considerable amount of vocational funds was utilized for research and for exemplary projects designed to develop and implement career education.

Bilingual Vocational Education

In section 191 of the 1974 education amendments, Congress published a "statement of findings," and in a very real sense pointed out an acute need: that of the many youths and adults who cannot profit from vocational education because of their limited ability to deal with the English language. These individuals are unable to fill the critical need for more and better trained personnel in vital occupational categories. Further, Congress emphasized the critical shortage of instructors who were skilled in both the job requirements and in languages—English as well as the native speech of the vocational students.

The U.S. Commissioner of Education and the Secretary of Labor were given joint responsibility to:

1. Develop and disseminate accurate information on the status of bilingual vocational training in the United States
2. Evaluate the impact of such bilingual vocational training on employment and underemployment.

Congress authorized $17.5 million for the fiscal year 1975 to carry out the necessary research required under this section of the law. Grants and contracts were utilized as the means whereby the Commissioner could accomplish the intent and purpose of this section of the law.

Summary

The Education Amendments of 1972 is truly an omnibus educational enactment. Of particular importance, within the limitations of this law, is the potential for growth of vocational or occupational education at all levels, from the elementary education programs in our public schools to the institutions of higher education. Likewise, the potential for a nationally coordinated research effort aimed at uncovering many of the mysteries of the teaching-learning process was made possible through this enactment.

The Education Amendments of 1974 sought to consolidate and refine previous legislation. Like the 1972 Amendments, this piece of legislation provided specific priority areas for vocational educators. The Women's Educational Equality Act sought to open up many educational programs to women which had previously been unavailable to them primarily because of traditional methods of operation.

That section dealing with individualized educational plans for special needs students has provided the impetus necessary to bring vocational educators together in working toward a common goal, that of preparing students for the world of work.

Career education was identified as a movement that was highly desirable and worthy of separate funding and that should not be dependent upon the funds allocated to vocational education for research and development activities. These sections of the law have caused vocational educators to reevaluate their program offerings and their methods of coordinating educational programs with those of other professionals within each LEA.

Bilingual vocational education programs continue to be a problem. However, research and exemplary projects are seeking some solutions to the need for providing bilingual vocational education programs for persons with language handicaps who desire to move into the mainstream of American society.

Questions for Review

1. What factors have impeded progress toward implementation of many of the Parts provided for or included in the Education Amendments of 1972?

2. What is the significance of the 1202 Commissions, as described in the Act?

3. Who was responsible for assuring that "industrial arts" was included in Title II of the Amendments?

4. What is the major purpose for the NIE as described in the Education Amendments of 1972?

5. What other legislative enactment was aimed primarily at educational research?

6. Who must be involved in the development of the Individualized Educational Plans (IEP)s?

7. What social factors brought about the need for the Women's Educational Equality Act?

8. What impact will career education have upon vocational programs and what is the source of funding for career education?

9. What is the critical need identified for bilingual vocational education programs?

Suggested Activities

1. Interview representatives of local postsecondary education agencies. Determine their feelings regarding the major emphasis placed on community colleges under the Education Amendments.

2. Determine what groups in your state have been, or are seeking to be, appointed as the 1202 Commission. Based on their past history, describe how you think they would guide postsecondary education.

3. Procure a copy of the Bill entitled the *Occupational Education Act of 1971* (S. 1856 and/or H.R. 7429). Identify the various parts of these proposed enactments that are found in the Education Amendments of 1972.

4. Discuss the importance, in your opinion, of the establishment of a Bureau of Occupational and Adult Education at the Federal level.

5. Prepare a personal file on the National Institute of Education (NIE). Try to obtain various requests for proposals (RFPs) that are sent out by this agency.

6. Determine whether there is a common denominator regarding the type of research funded by the NIE.

7. Arrange a meeting with a special education teacher to prepare a sample IEP.

8. If you have special needs students in your class or school, attend at least one "staffing" meeting in which the IEP is discussed with those parties who are to be involved.

9. Identify and explain the social factors which have brought about a greater concern for women's education equality.

10. Conduct a mini needs assessment to determine the number of people who could profit from bilingual vocational education programs in your local area.

Bibliography

Alford, A. L. "Education's New Landmark Legislation." *American Education* 8 (7) (August and September 1972): 4.

Beckler, J. "Side Skirmish in the Battle Over Education Amendments of 1972." *School Management* 7 (September 1972): 8.

_____. "Washington Report." *School Management* 8 (1) (January 1973): 11.

_____. "At Long Last Congress Recognizes the Needs of Higher Education." *College Management* 7 (August 1972): 7.

Cosand, J. P. "Power of Collective Response." *Educational Record* 53 (Fall 1972): 270.

Davis, J. R. "Higher Education Amendments of 1972: A New Form Of Aid For Private Colleges and Universities?" *INTELLECT* 101 (December 1972): 157.

Marland, S. P. "Federal Role in Community Education." *Phi Delta Kappan* 54 (November 1972): 146.

P. L. 93-380 Education Amendments of 1974, 20 USC 821.

Schuchat, T. "From Washington." *School Shop* 32 (1) (September 1972): 104.

Strassenburg, A. A. "National and Legislative News: Education Amendments of 1972." *Journal of College Science Teaching* 2 (1) (October 1972): 10.

Van Valkenburg, J. "What The 1972 Education Amendments Offer The Private College." *College Management* 7 (September 1972): 8.

Wentworth, Eric. "The Higher Education Act—And Beyond." *Change,* 4 (7) (September 1972): 63.

Notes and Revisions

7

Education Amendments of 1976:
Current Federal Support for Vocational Education

Objectives

- The student will describe the primary components of the Education Amendments of 1976.
- The student will analyze the vocational education titles of the Education Amendments of 1976.
- The student will compare and contrast the various parts and sections of the vocational education titles with prior vocational education legislation.

Introduction

As described in chapter 6, national level legislators and administrators were committed to writing omnibus and comprehensive legislative enactments related to education. This was reinforced when congress passed the Education Amendments of 1976 (PL. 94-482) and when it was signed into law by President Gerald R. Ford, October 12, 1976. An extension and revision of prior vocational education legislation was included. Likewise other titles were included. Higher Education, Career Education, Guidance and Counseling, Adult Education, Community Colleges and Post-secondary Planning, and many other concerns were addressed.

71

Table 7-1. VOCATIONAL EDUCATION AUTHORIZATIONS EDUCATION AMENDMENTS OF 1976

(The Vocational Education Act of 1963 as Amended 1976)

Program	FY 78	FY 79	FY 80	FY 81	FY 82
Basic State Grants (Sec. 120) Including: Sex Bias Monitoring Personnel (Sec. 104(b)) ($50,000 per state) Work-Study (Sec. 121) Cooperative Education (Sec. 122) Energy Education (Sec. 123) Residential Schools (Sec. 124)	$ 704,000,000	$ 824,000,000	$ 944,000,000	$1,060,000,000	$1,188,000,000
Program Improvement and Supportive Services (Sec. 130) Including: Research (Sec. 131) Exemplary and Innovative (Sec. 132) Curriculum Development (Sec. 133) Guidance and Counseling (Sec. 134) Pre-Service and In-Service Training (Sec. 135) Grants to Reduce Sex Bias (Sec. 136)	176,000,000	206,000,000	236,000,000	265,000,000	297,000,000

Table 7-1. VOCATIONAL EDUCATION AUTHORIZATIONS EDUCATION AMENDMENTS OF 1976 (continued)

(The Vocational Education Act of 1963 as Amended 1976)

Program	FY 78	FY 79	FY 80	FY 81	FY 82
State Planning Grants	25,000,000	25,000,000	25,000,000	25,000,000	25,000,000
Special Disadvantaged (Sec. 140)	35,000,000	40,000,000	45,000,000	50,000,000	50,000,000
Consumer and Homemaking (Sec. 150)	55,000,000	65,000,000	75,000,000	80,000,000	80,000,000
Bilingual Training (Sec. 181)	60,000,000	70,000,000	80,000,000	90,000,000	80,000,000
Renovation and Remodeling (Sec. 191) (Urban and Rural)	25,000,000	50,000,000	75,000,000	100,000,000	
State Advisory Councils (Sec. 105)	8,000,000	8,500,000	9,000,000	10,000,000	8,000,000
National Advisory Council (Sec. 162)	450,000	475,000	500,000	500,000	500,000
TOTALS	$1,088,450,000	$1,288,975,000	$1,489,500,000	$1,680,500,000	$1,703,500,000

General Provisions of PL. 94-482

Title I of the Education Amendments of 1976 deals primarily with higher education programs and management. This title was divided into nine major parts. Included were:

Part A. Community Services and Continuing Education

Part B. College Library Assistance and Library Training and Research

Part C. Strengthening Developing Institutions

Part D. Student Assistance

Part E. Education Professions Development

Part F. Financial Assistance for the Improvement of Undergraduate Instruction

Part G. Construction of Academic Facilities

Part H. Graduate Programs

Part I. Community Colleges and State Post-secondary Planning

Part J. General Provisions

Of particular interest to occupational and career education professionals is Part D, which defines specific sources of student financial assistance.

Title II of the 1976 Amendments amends the Vocational Education Act of 1963. Categorical funding, while significantly reduced under the 1968 VEA, is further reduced under the provisions of PL. 94-482. The Amendments of 1976 can be functionally subdivided into ten primary components: Part A (sub parts 1-5), State Vocational Education Programs; Part B (sub parts 1-4), National Programs; and Part C, Definitions. A careful review of the funding patterns authorized by this legislation will indicate the strength of the established priorities. In order to carry out the provisions of the act, Congress authorized to be appropriated the following funds in the various categories. (The reader is cautioned to remember that there are considerable differences between the amount authorized and the amounts of money actually appropriated for a given year). See Table 7-1.

Part A   State Vocational Education Programs

Part A, Section 102, provided a very clear statement of purpose for this piece of legislation and reflects congressional concern for state vocational education programs in several major areas: comprehensive planning, which includes input from non-education; elimination of sex discrimination and sex stereotyping; and evaluation of program effectiveness. Emphasis was also given to learners with special educational needs. An in-depth review of this and companion legislation will appear in a later chapter. This category provided that each state assign higher priority to integrating the special-needs learners into regular vocational programs.

The Act provided that each state shall, consistent with state law, designate a board or agency to be the state agency responsible for administration or supervision of the administration of all public vocational programs within the state.

Specific areas of concern were identified which have had an impact upon the operation of each state board and vocational education administrative structure. Administrative costs at the state level are to be shared equally by the state and federal governments. A two year phase-in of this provision was allowed. Therefore, many states, for the first time, must contribute funds on a 50-50 basis with the federal government for the administration of vocational education. This is an important section, for this very basic provision tests the willingness of state governments to assume their responsibility for providing vocational programs.

A further provision under Part A, state administrative responsibilities, is the development and submission of a five-year plan. The development of five-year plans must involve persons at all educational levels who have concerns or interests in vocational education. This includes persons on secondary, post-secondary, community and junior college, or higher education levels; representatives of local school boards or committees; vocational education teachers; local school administrators, and manpower services council personnel. All are to be actively involved in the preparation of the plan. Also to be included in this planning group is a representative from the state agency responsible for private non-profit and proprietary institutions that offer programs at less than the baccalaureate degree level. Additionally, the state advisory council on vocational education is to be an active participant in the five-year-plan development. The above list of representatives from the various state educational agencies is a clear indication that Congress intends vocational education to be based on comprehensive planning. It is particularly interesting to note the inclusion of a manpower planning council representative because this group is responsible for state and regional planning under the U.S. Department of Labor's CETA program.

The legislation provides a detailed process which must be followed in developing the five-year plan. During the planning year, at least four meetings must be held with the above-mentioned representatives. The plan for this series of meetings is as follows: The first meeting shall be held prior to development of the five-year plan; the second meeting shall be to review and discuss the first draft of the plan; the third meeting will review again the rewritten plan that resulted from the previous meeting ; the fourth meeting is designated as the approved meeting at which the representatives shall give their approval of the final draft of the five-year plan. The state board has the responsibility for final approval of all provisions of the five-year plan. However, included with the plan must be:

1. The recommendations rejected by the board
2. The agency, council or individual making the recommendations
3. The reasons the state board rejected the recommendations.

An agency, council, or individual also has the right to appeal the decision of the state board to the U.S. Commissioner of Education.

The state board must also hold a series of public hearings in every region of the state to permit all segments of the population to give their views of the needs of vocational education. Goals, courses to be taught, and the allocation of local state and federal resources to meet these goals are open for review and discussion. The state plan must then include the views and concerns presented at the hearings, with a description of how the state plan addresses these concerns.

In developing the five-year plan, the Planning Committee must assess the current and future job requirements for the state and region. This information must include present and projected employment needs. The Committee must also outline the specific goals the state will seek to accomplish by the end of the five-year period and give a detailed description of methods to be utilized in accomplishing these goals, including courses to be taught, projected enrollments, allocation of responsibility and the allotment of local, state, and federal funds among the various levels of education throughout the state.

Annual Program Plans

Each state must also submit to the Commissioner an annual program plan and accountability report for each fiscal year. In formulating this plan and report the State Board must actively involve the representatives of the agencies, councils, etc., who are required to participate in the development of the five-year plan. Again, specific provisions have been made in regard to the number of meetings required and the hearing process. The state board has essentially the same responsibility for the annual plan as it has in developing the five-year plan.

The accountability report which is to accompany the annual plan may have caused the greatest amount of concern for vocational administrators at all educational levels. The law is quite specific in some areas, while other areas of program operation appear to be quite nebulous. For example, the accountability report is required to show the results of coordination of programs funded under this Act with those of manpower training programs. Also the accountability report must indicate compliance with the provision of equal access to programs by both men and women. In other areas of concern, which generally are considered a part of the accountability movement, considerably less direction is provided. Therefore, each state annual report must indicate explicitly the degree to which the state achieved the goals and complied with the use of funds as outlined in the five-year plan. Each must also indicate how funds have been used as authorized by this act for basic grants, program improvement, and supportive services, special programs for the disadvantaged and handicapped and other special service areas of the act. A later section of this chapter will provide more detail regarding the requirements of the accountability report.

The second major component of Education Amendments of 1976 concerns sex bias and sex stereotyping. Virtually every section of Title II refers to the necessity of eliminating sex bias and sex stereotyping in vocational education. Special categorical funding of the law requires that states use $50,000.00 and designate full-time personnel with the specific responsibility of assisting state and local personnel in eliminating sex bias and sex stereotyping in vocational education. Every aspect of vocational education is included in this new requirement.

This is an area of concern which has been a priority of Congress for many years. Title VII of the Civil Rights Act of 1964 provides the basis for the current legislative enactments.

The rights of women in the work force and their right to vocational education programs were given high priority in the Education Amendments of 1972. Title IX of these amendments is aimed at eliminating sex discrimination and sex role stereotyping in vocational education. Title IX states "no person shall . . . on the basis of sex, be excluded from participation in, be denied the benefits of or be subjected to discrimination under any educational program or activity receiving federal financial assistance." Because of this high priority and concern, the Committee on Education and Labor held separate hearings on sex discrimination and sex stereotyping in vocational education. The Committee concluded that the inferior position women held in the labor market is being reinforced by many current practices in vocational education.

According to testimony before the House Committee on Education and Labor, female enrollments in vocational education accounted for 55 percent of vocational education enrollments in 1972. Furthermore, most females enrolled were concentrated in a narrow range of courses that were in female-intensive and low-paying occupations. At the same time, males enrolled in vocational education programs had three times as many options open to them in male-intensive programs as women had in female-intensive programs.

A comparison of pay for traditional women's occupations with traditional men's occupations find that women are woefully behind. Labor statistics suggest that if women are to raise their pay, they must seek out non-traditional occupations—that is, those occupations which are dominated by males. The House Committee on Education and Labor concluded that vocational education is doing little to improve the lot of women. The Education Amendments of 1976 provide that each state must develop and implement policies and procedures which will assure equal access to vocational education programs by both women and men. The state plan must provide: (1) a detailed description of such policies and procedures (2) actions to be taken to overcome sex discrimination and sex stereotyping in all state and local vocational education programs, and (3) incentives, to be provided to eligible recipients to encourage enrollment of both women and men in non-traditional courses of study and to develop model programs to reduce sex stereotyping in all occupations.

The elimination of sex bias and sex stereotyping as a priority for vocational education will cause many vocational teachers and administrators to evaluate course and program prerequisites, because sex can no longer be a criteria for entrance into the many vocational programs. The job of equalizing enrollment and subsequent employment is enormous. Socialization and tradition is so pervasive and ingrained that sex bias and discrimination will be practiced at a subconcious level. Continued emphasis will, however, provide the impetus for change.

Evaluation of Vocational Programs

Program planning and evaluation received considerable emphasis in the 1976 amendments. Several major areas of concern were identified. First, a data system at the state and national level is to be developed. This system is to have uniform definitions which will contain elements descriptive of vocational education students, programs, program completers and leavers, staff, facilities, and expenditures. The purpose of such a data system is to assist in planning and to assess the extent that state and local programs are enabling students to secure employment in their field. Congress learned in testimony taken prior to the enactment of this legislation, that the available vocational education data were not compatible from state to state. Thus the charge to develop a nationally uniform data reporting and accounting system.

In addition to the newly mandated standardized data system, Congress also sought to strengthen the vocational programs and to assist the agencies in operating the best possible programs. In order to accomplish this, each state must evaluate the effectiveness of all programs within the state that are receiving funds under the 1976 Vocational Education Act. The results of these evaluations shall be used to revise the states' vocational education programs. The effectiveness of the various vocational programs shall be determined according to the extent to which program completers and leavers: (1) find employment in occupations related to their training, and (2) are considered by their employers to be well-trained and prepared for employment. Pursuit of additional education or training by program completers or leavers cannot be considered negatively in these evaluations.

The state advisory councils have a more active role in the evaluation phase. Each state board must consult with the state advisory council on an annual basis and shall assist the state in developing the evaluation plans and in monitoring the evaluations conducted by the state, and shall use the evaluations in compiling the annual report. The state advisory council is required to submit its annual evaluation report to the U.S. Commissioner and to the national advisory council.

The evaluation process is an effort to determine the effectiveness of vocational programs, services, and activities during the year under review. The basis for this evaluation shall be the program goals and objectives specified in the five-year state plan.

Beginning October 1, 1977, at least ten states each fiscal year will be evaluated by the Bureau of Occupational and Adult Education. The purpose of this review shall be to analyze the strengths and weaknesses of the programs receiving federal funds. At the same time the Department of Health, Education and Welfare will conduct fiscal audits of programs in these same states.

The federal government is taking a more active role in the operation of vocational programs at the state and local level. The provisions for program review and evaluation address several problem areas namely, the need for: (1) a uniform data collection and reporting system, with clearly specified and agreed upon definitions (2) a systematic review by each state of programs which are designed to meet the goals and objectives specified in the five-year state plan (effectiveness of the multitude of vocational programs shall be determined by the number of students who find employment and who are considered well trained by employers; also by the number of students who pursue additional education); and (3) periodic review of each state's programs, to determine the overall strengths and weaknesses, by the Bureau of Occupational and Adult Education.

Part B   National Vocational Education Programs

Part B of the 1976 VEA addresses the specifics related to national programs or the Commissioner's Discretionary Programs. Under the General Provisions, there has been established in the Office of Education, a Bureau of Occupational and Adult Education. This office is headed by the Deputy Commissioner and has the responsibility for administration of all vocational and career education programs funded by this or any other act of Congress which fall within the authority of the Commissioner. These include programs dealing with manpower and training, for which the Commissioner has responsibility: post-secondary vocational, technical and occupational training, and career education.

In order to carry out the provisions of this legislation, the Bureau of Occupational and Adult Education was allocated 13 new positions. In each of the three grade-level positions specified, one or more workers were to be persons who had broad experience in the fields of junior and community college education, private proprietary education, and occupational guidance and counseling, or who were skilled workers in a recognized occupation. In addition, at least two positions were to be filled by persons on a subprofessional technician level in a social or medical services occupation. These individuals would serve as senior advisors in the administration of programs in the Bureau.

Vocational Education Data and Occupational Information Data Systems

In testimony that preceded the enactment of this legislation, a common complaint was that vocational education data were not compatible across states, and hence that aggregation of it at the federal level was of questionable validity as an indicator of the general status of vocational education. Given the pervasiveness of the problem and the harmony of voices raised in protest of the lack of adequate data, Congress responded by mandating the establishment of a nationally uniform data reporting and accounting system. (Drewes, 1978)

In order to bring about standardization of the data, Congress directed that the initial step in the development of this system be the development of uniform definitions. These definitions were to be developed jointly by the U.S. Commissioner's office and the Administrator of the National Center for Educational Statistics. Once developed, these definitions would serve as the basis for reporting and evaluating vocational education programs throughout the nation.

The Vocational Education Data System must include information regarding:

1. Students' enrollment (including information on their race and sex)
2. Programs
3. Program completers and leavers
4. Staff
5. Facilities
6. Expenditures

The program completers and leavers provision of this Act has brought about the greatest area of concern for vocational teachers and administrators. All state vocational education programs purporting to impart entry level job skills, and receiving assistance under the Act are to be evaluated according to the extent that program completers and leavers find employment in occupations related to their training and are considered by their employers to be well-trained and prepared for employment. This requirement, coupled with the requirement that evaluation data be included as a part of each annual plan, made standardized outcome measures a reality. While this is but one example of a standardized outcome measure, it should be noted that the Act does provide that program completers and leavers who pursue further education should not be counted in a negative manner.

In carrying out an expanding monitoring role of vocational education programs, Congress has provided that the flow of standardized outcome data shall come from the local labor market areas of each state, through the state administrative agency to the federal level.

In developing the vocational education data system (VEDS), Congress also specified that wherever possible this system would be compatible with information systems involving data on programs assisted under the Comprehensive Employment and Training Act (CETA) 1973.

The U.S. Commissioner of Education is required to submit an annual report to Congress concerning the status of vocational education. To assure an independent evaluation of the state of vocational education, the National Institute of Education has been directed by Congress to conduct a thorough evaluation of vocational education at the state and local levels and to report its findings to the President and Congress no later than September 30, 1980.

National Occupational Information Data System

Continued emphasis has been placed upon coordinating activities of all federal programs which provide occupational education and training. The National Occupational Information Coordrinating Committee was established under Part B, Section 161 (b) of this Act. Membership consists of the U.S. Commissioner of Education, the Deputy Commissioner of the Bureau of Occupational and Adult Education, the Commissioner of Labor Statistics, and the Assistant Secretary for Employment and Training. The Committee is charged with the responsibility:

1. To improve coordination between and communication among administrators and planners of the 1976 VEA Act, and professionals charged with   similar responsibility for CETA legislation
2. To develop and implement an occupational information system to meet common occupational information needs of vocational education programs and employment and training programs at national, state, and local levels.

Each state, with funds made available from the National Coordinating Committee, must implement an occupational information system which will meet the planning and operation needs of vocational education and CETA programs within the state. A state Occupational Information Coordinating Committee composed of representatives of the State Board, State Employment Security Agency, State Manpower Services Council, and the agency administering vocational rehabilitation programs, has the responsibility for the state occupational information system.

National Advisory Council on Vocational Education

The National Advisory Council on Vocational Education established with the Vocational Education Act of 1963 continues to exist with the Vocational Education Amendments of 1976. The major deviations from previous legislation are the stipulations that the majority of its members be non-educators and that representation on the committee be appropriate for the categories specified. The National Advisory Council has been expanded to 21 members and shall include individuals representative of:

1. Labor and management
2. New and emerging occupations
3. Vocational guidance
4. National Commission for Manpower Policy
5. Nonprofit private schools
6. Women with background and experiences in employment and training programs, who are knowledgeable with respect to administration of state and local vocational programs
7. Administration of state and local vocational education programs (including members of school boards and private institutions)
8. Experienced educators of the handicapped
9. Persons familiar with the problems of the disadvantaged

10. Persons knowledgeable about post-secondary and adult vocational education programs
11. Correctional institutions
12. The general public who are not federal employees.

The purpose of the Council is to advise the President, Congress, Secretary, and Commissioner concerning the administration, preparation of general regulations, and budget requests for operation of vocational education programs.

Professional Development for Vocational Education Personnel

Significant changes were made in the Educational Amendments of 1976 in the area of professional development for vocational education personnel. Part B, Section 172 provided the Commissioner with funds to provide educational opportunities for professionals. Types of opportunities listed were for:

1. Experienced vocational educators, to spend full-time in advanced study of vocational education, not to exceed three years
2. Certified teachers who have been trained to teach in other fields to become vocational educators if they have experience and skills in a vocational field
3. Persons in industry who have skills and experience in vocational fields in which there is a need for vocational educators, but who do not necessarily have a baccalaureate degree.

This section of the Act has had significant impact upon the individual vocational education professional, on the State Department of Education, and on institutions of higher education. There has been a reduction in the number of institutions which have been approved as vocational education leadership development institutions. Furthermore, to the maximum degree possible, fellowships are to be granted to persons seeking to become vocational teachers in areas identified as needing additional teachers now and in the future.

Bilingual Vocational Training

A continued area of concern on the part of Congress is bilingual vocational education, Part B, Section 181. Congress found this to be an acute problem in the United States involving millions of citizens both children and adults. Many individuals are unable to profit from vocational education because of limited English-speaking ability. These individuals are unable to fill the need for more and better educated personnel in vital occupational categories. In addition, these same individuals suffer the hardship of unemployment or underemployment. The critical need in this area is vocational instructors who have job skills and knowledge as well as dual language capabilities. Under the provisions of this section of the Act, the Commissioner must determine the status of bilingual vocational programs, and determine the impact of bilingual vocational training on the shortages of well-trained personnel.

In order to bring about the desired changes in this particular area, the Commissioner is authorized to make grants and to make contracts with state and local education agencies and private nonprofit vocational training institutions in order to provide training in recognized and new occupations. Instruction in the English language must also be provided where English is essential for success once the student enters the world of work.

Grants and contracts may be used to provide vocational education for the following individuals:

1. Persons who have completed or left elementary schools and who are available for education by a post-secondary educational institution
2. Persons who have already entered the labor market, who desire and need training or retraining to achieve year-round employment, adjust to changing manpower needs, expand their range of skills, or advance in employment
3. Participants in bilingual vocational training programs subject to the same conditions and limitations as are set forth in Section 111 of the Comprehensive Employment and Training Act of 1973.

This section of the Act re-emphasizes the same concern for bilingual vocational education found in the Education Amendments of 1974.

Subpart 4—Emergency Assistance for Remodeling and Renovation of Vocational Education Facilities, makes specific reference to the Architectural Barriers Act of 1968. Through the provisions of this section of the VEA, monies have been authorized to assist LEAs in remodeling and renovations which will make all vocational education facilities accessible to handicapped persons. This provision is designed to assist all schools in meeting the Architectural Barriers Act as well as PL 94-142 Education for All Handicapped Children Act of 1975.

Summary

The education amendments of 1976, Title II, brought about many changes in the Vocational Education Act of 1963. New funding categories were added and significant changes were made in some of the existing categories. Administrative costs were to be shared equally by state and federal government. There was an increase in the set-aside monies for the disadvantaged and handicapped.

Program planning and operation at the state level was given a mandate for comprehensive planning, with annual and long-range plans now a major activity for each administrative unit. Further, each state was to designate a single state board which was to be responsible for the administration of vocational education. This comprehensive planning process must involve a wider range of people, with considerable effort being directed toward the coordination of vocational education programs and the Comprehensive Employment and Training Act programs.

Nearly every section of the act contained provisions for the elimination of sex discrimination and sex stereotyping in vocational education. This has been a major concern of legislators since the civil rights act of 1964. However, there is little evidence to indicate that substantial progress is being made.

At the national level, the most important change, and one which will have immediate impact upon local and state program operation, is the development of the Vocational Education Data System, which will bring about some standardization and systematic evaluation of vocational programs in all states.

Questions for Review

1. What factors have impeded the elimination of sex discrimination and sex stereotyping in vocational programs?

2. What are the implications of the mandated coordination between vocational education programs and CETA programs?

3. How is the $50,000.00 grant to each state for sex discrimination and sex stereotyping to be used?

4. What criteria is to be used for program evaluation?

5. Who is charged with the responsibility for developing the Vocational Education Data System?

Suggested Activities

1. Interview a local school administrator to determine the numbers of students enrolling in female or male intensive occupational programs.

2. Obtain a state plan for vocational education and identify the evaluation procedures and the system for coordinating vocational education and CETA programs.

3. What, in your opinion, is the importance of a standardized reporting system for vocational education?

4. Interview a local vocational education administrator to determine how the linkages between CETA and vocational education have been established.

Bibliography

American Vocational Journal. "Provisions of the New Vocational Education Amendments." November 1976, p. 33–35.

Ellis, M. L. "Sexism in Vocational Education." *Industrial Education,* October 1976.

Gilbreath, J. D., "Sex Discrimination and Title VII of the Civil Rights Act." *Personnel Journal,* January 1977, p. 23–26.

Hill, P. T. "Title I Under the Microscope." *American Education,* October 1976.

Jennings, J. F. "Emerging Issues in Vocational Education." *American Vocational Journal,* December 1975, p. 29–32.

P.L. 94–482, Educational Amendments of 1976.

Reid, J. L. "Involvement to Ensure Quality Is the Name of the Game." *American Vocational Journal,* November 1976, p. 30-32.

U.S. Office of Education. *The Handbook: A Vocational Education Legislative Reference.* U.S. Department of Health, Education and Welfare, January 1978.

8

Career Education for the Handicapped: *A New Partnership*

Objectives

- The student will review the legislation concerning the handicapped and will identify the major provisions.
- The student will define "vocational education" as referred to in PL 94–142.
- The student will describe some relationships among Education for All Handicapped Children Act, Section 504 of the Vocational Rehabilitation Act, and the Vocational Amendments of 1976.
- The student will describe the effect these legislative enactments have had on current occupational and career education programs.

Introduction

Education for all has long been an American goal; however, all individuals have not always been able to participate in public education programs. The discrepancy between stated goals and what actually exists is not new. What is new is the amount of current interest in reducing this discrepancy. As a result of the civil rights movement of the 1950s and 1960s and the Civil Rights Act of 1964, equal opportunity in education has become a national concern. This concern has resulted in additional legislation and litigation to insure that equal opportunity in education applies also to handicapped persons.

In this chapter, the recent legislation, which affects the operation of the nation's elementary, secondary, and post-secondary institutions, will be discussed. A new partnership has been formed with the passage of the Education for All Handicapped Children Act of 1975 (PL 94-142); the Education Amendments of 1976 (PL 94-482), which amend the Vocational Education Act of 1963; and the Rehabilitation Act of 1973, Sections 503 and 504 (PL 93-112). The primary goal of these pieces of legislation is to provide the handicapped with effective vocational programming; the anticipated outcome being well adjusted, suitably employed handicapped citizens. As will be noted when each specific act is examined in detail, these three legislative enactments provide an education continuum from age three through the adult years.

The rationale for this legislation is well documented. The President's committee on employment of the handicapped reported that the work records of handicapped persons compare favorably with those of the nonhandicapped. Unfortunately, the employment and training oppor- tunities in the vocational schools as well as in the work places of the nation are not equally available to the handicapped and non-handi- capped. In a typical year, 40 percent of all disabled adults will be employed, compared with 75 percent of the non-disabled population (Levitan, 1976). During fiscal year 1976 only 1.7% of the total vocational education enrollment was identified as handicapped (Lee, 1975), and 70 percent of those individuals identified as handicapped were placed in separate classes (Olympus Research Corp., 1974). Additional evidence has been presented in the numerous publications dealing with the problems of the handicapped, and the statistics presented support the need for an expansion of vocational programs to include those for handicapped individuals.

In response to the obvious, Congress has responded with three legislative enactments designed to meet the needs of all handicapped individuals.

The Education of All Handicapped Children Act of 1975 (PL 94-142)

With the passage of PL 94-142, the Education for All Handicapped Children Act of 1975, Congress mandated a national special education law charging state and local education agencies with the responsibility of providing free and appropriate education for all handicapped children ages 3–21. Congress in its deliberations found that on a national level the needs of handicapped children were not being met. Of approximately eight million handicapped children in the United States more than half do not receive appropriate educational services, and nearly one million handicapped children are excluded entirely from the public school system. Many handicapped children participating in regular school programs have undetected handicaps which prevent them from being successful in their educational programs. Congress also found that because of the lack of adequate services within the public school system, families are often forced to find services elsewhere at their own expense. Congress found that if given appropriate funding, state and local educational agencies were capable of providing the services required to meet the needs of handicapped children.

In specifying that *free* and *appropriate* public education be available to all handicapped children, the Act provides several assurances and protective measures for handicapped learners and their parents. The following assurances must be provided at the state and local education agency level:

1. A guarantee of complete due process procedure
2. Assurance that written, individualized educational plans will be developed and maintained for each student
3. Assurance that each student will be served in the "least restrictive educational environment" (This requires that, to the maximum extent, appropriate, handicapped learners be educated with non-handicapped learners; that restrictive environments, such as special classes or special schools, should only be utilized when the nature or severity of the handicap is such that supplementary services and aids provided in the regular classes are not effective.)
4. Assurance that testing and evaluation materials and procedures utilized for placement of handicapped children be selected and administered so as not to be racially or culturally discriminatory
5. Assurance that policies and procedures to protect the confidentiality of student records be provided.

Based upon the "authorizing" mechanism, Congress established the following expenditures for carrying out the provisions of this Act:

Fiscal Year	1978	387 million (5%)
	1979	775 million (10%)
	1980	1.2 billion (20%)
	1981	2.32 billion (30%)
	1982	3.16 billion (40%)

The above amounts represent percentages of the average expenditures per pupil in public elementary and secondary schools in the United States. In determining the allotment for each state, the commissioner may count only 12 percent of the total school age population of the state, ages 5–17 inclusive.

Several specific provisions, which directly affect vocational education of the handicapped are also found in PL 94–142. First, Section 613 (a)(2), which deals with state plans submitted to the U.S. Office of Education, provides that programs and procedures are to be established to assure that funds received by the state under any other federal program, including the Vocational Education Act of 1963, will be used in a manner consistent with the goal of providing a free and appropriate public education for all handicapped children. Since it was determined that "appropriate education" must include a written individualized educational program (IEP), handicapped students enrolled in regular, and special education classes will have IEPs. Vocational teachers then must have an active role in the development of IEPs.

A second major link between PL 94-142 and vocational education programs is established under the full educational opportunity goal. The legislation specifically states that ". . . state and local agencies shall take steps to insure that handicapped children have available to them the variety of programs and services available to non-handicapped children, including . . . industrial arts, home economics and vocational education." It should be noted that this legislation has expanded the educational opportunities for special education or handicapped students because all programs, including industrial arts, home economics, and vocational education, must be made available.

The role of vocational education in the education of handicapped persons at secondary and post-secondary institutions has been expanded and is crucial to the career preparation of these students. This being the case, provisions for developing the individualized educational plans (IEPs) must include a joint effort on the part of the vocational teacher, special education teacher and all others specifically mentioned. If a determination is made that the student is deficient in pre-vocational and vocational skills and is in need of remediation, short and long range instructional objectives, including time lines and criteria for evaluation, are to be included in the IEP.

A comprehensive system of personnel development is to be included in each state plan to facilitate the implementation of the provisions of this Act. Inservice and preservice training activities must be provided to insure that all instructional personnel be adequately prepared to deal with the specific educational requirements of the handicapped. Funds to provide inservice and follow-up technical assistance are provided in the Act. Such personnel would include, but not be limited to, regular, special, and vocational educators, career guidance counselors, work-study coordinators and job placement personnel.

A very real implication of PL 94-142 is a demand for greater cooperation and coordination among all areas of teacher education—vocational, regular, and special, including the practicing professionals at the local school level. Educational professionals must work together to incorporate these changes into teacher education programs.

The Education Amendments of 1976
(PL 94-482)

Title II of this Act, as in previous vocational legislation, specifies that 10 percent of the federal vocational education general program funds must be spent on vocational education for the handicapped. These set-aside funds must now be matched by state and local funds. Thus, the Act has doubled the total amount of money available for education of the handicapped. Additional provisions have also been made in regard to the use of these monies. First, to the maximum extent possible, handicapped students are to be placed in regular vocational programs. Also the monies received must be used for excess costs, that is, costs above and beyond the costs of providing vocational education to non-handicapped students.

Public Law 94-482 also has the requirement, and expresses the concern of Congress, that those provisions relating to the preparation of handicapped individuals be consistent and considered in conjunction with PL 94-142 and Section 503 and 504 of the Rehabilitation Act of 1973.

Those states which wish to receive federal vocational education funds must specify in their five-year plan:

1. How the vocational programs for handicapped students are consistent with the state plan requirements under the Education for All Handicapped Children Act of 1975 (PL 94–142) and that the goals of vocational education are consistent with the goals of PL 94-142.

2. How the programs and services to be provided each handicapped student will be planned and coordinated with the student's individualized educational program. This means the vocational education teacher will be developing the vocational education portion of the individualized plan.

The vocational amendments also require that each state advisory council for vocational education have at least one member who is knowledgeable about the special education needs of handicapped persons. The Education for All Handicapped Children Act also mandates a state advisory panel for handicapped persons. The primary purpose of representation on state advisory councils is to insure that coordination between vocational and special needs education takes place. These two acts complement each other and are to be implemented in concert with the Rehabilitation Act of 1973.

The Rehabilitation Act of 1973
Sections 503 and 504 (PL 93-112)

The rights of handicapped persons in the work place received attention under the rehabilitation act of 1973. Sections 503 and 504 emphasize these rights. While many businesses have hired handicapped individuals in the past, other employers have excluded the handicapped either consciously or unconsciously. The rehabilitation acts are civil rights acts and are every bit as powerful as the Civil Rights Act of 1964. Since they are civil rights acts, no age limits have been established for the handicapped persons covered. No funds were authorized for implementation of the provisions. However, there has been considerable effort made to coordinate the services of education agencies and vocational rehabilitation agencies.

Section 503 of the rehabilitation act deals with affirmative action guidelines for employers with federal contracts of more than $2,500.00. Employers with such contracts must take affirmative action to hire handicapped people. If the contracts or subcontracts involve more than $50,000.00 and 50 or more persons are employed, the contractor must develop an affirmative action program listing recruitment procedures and sources from which handicapped persons will be recruited. While no time lines or quotas have been established, the employers are required to make "reasonable accommodations" for all handicapped persons interested in employment. "Reasonable accommodation" is to be determined by a review of the employer's affirmative action program. A primary emphasis in this section of the Act is placed on encouraging employers to hire the handicapped.

It is logical that businesses and industries, in their effort to recruit handicapped persons, will be looking to local vocational education programs for assistance. With the implementation of placement services provided under PL 94-482, better linkages between business and industry should develop and thus, better placement of the handicapped in the world of work.

Section 504 prohibits discrimination on the basis of handicaps in any private or public program or activity receiving federal financial assistance and is designed to bring handicapped persons into the mainstream of American life. This regulation requires agencies receiving federal assistance to do the following:

1. Provide opportunities, benefits, aids, or services for the handicapped equal to those provided the non-handicapped, even though these opportunities do not produce identical results or level of achievement for handicapped and non-handicapped persons
2. Provide aids, benefits, and services for the handicapped in the same setting as the non-handicapped except in cases where their effectiveness is jeopardized by doing so
3. Provide barrier-free environments to insure facility and program accessibility.
4. Equally recruit, train, promote, and compensate the handicapped.

The provisions of Section 503 and 504 have some very real implications for vocational education professionals at all levels. Each secondary school is required yearly to identify and locate every handicapped person in its district who is not getting a public education and to notify these persons of the school's obligation to provide services to them.

Post-secondary vocational education institutions are listed as agencies which will provide equal access for handicapped individuals. Modification of post-secondary vocational courses will be necessary with respect to time needed to complete the course requirements, teaching methods, and methods of conducting course examinations.

New construction in post-secondary facilities must provide accessibility for the handicapped. While not all existing facilities need to be accessible to handicapped students, alternative locations should be provided. Priority must be given to classes which provide the most integrated setting possible.

SUMMARY

A new partnership has been formed with the passage of these three pieces of legislation. Furthermore, the education and employment of the handicapped have been given the emphasis and priority needed to bring all handicapped persons into the mainstream of American life by providing a continuum of educational experiences from age 3 through adulthood. Cooperation and the coordination of activities have been incorporated into each of the laws, and state plans for implementation must be reviewed and found in compliance with the intent and purpose of each of the acts. The foundation has been laid for a new and better vocational education system which will enable the handicapped to become employed and productive. The fulfillment of the objectives will take the cooperation and efforts of all parties concerned with the needs and interests of handicapped persons.

Questions for Review

1. What, in your opinion, is the reason that handicapped workers are not hired at the same rate as non-handicapped?

2. What are the implications of education in the "least restrictive environment" and how might this affect the vocational teacher?

3. What is the purpose of the individualized instructional program, or IEP, and why should the vocational teacher assist in its development?

4. What provisions have been made in PL 94-482 to insure that coordination of activities occurs between vocational education and special education programs?

5. How will PL 93-112, the Rehabilitation Act of 1973, aid the cooperative vocational education coordinator?

Suggested Activities

1. Identify a special education teacher and ask to have the individualized educational program (IEP)'s process explained to you.

2. Obtain a state plan for vocational education and a state plan for the education of the handicapped and compare the provisions for education of handicapped in vocational programs.

3. Interview a school counselor or placement director to determine how handicapped students are identified and placed in the various vocational programs.

4. Conduct a case study and develop an individualized educational program for a handicapped person who will enroll in your vocational program.

5. Interview a personnel director of a major employer to determine how their affirmative action plan meets the needs of the handicapped.

Bibliography

Education Amendments of 1976, Public Law 94-482. Washington, D.C.: U.S. Government Printing Office, 1975.

Education for All Handicapped Children Act of 1975, Public Law 94-142. Washington, D.C.: U.S. Government Printing Office. 1975.

Holloran, W. D. "Handicapped Persons: Who are They?" *American Vocational Journal* 53-1:30-31.

Jones, R. "CETA's Problems with Hiring the Handicapped." *Work Life*. Washington, D.C.: Department of Labor, May 1977.

Lee, A. *Living a Learning Across the Nation*. Project Baseline, Vol. 4. Flagstaff: Northern Arizona University, 1975.

Levitan, S. A. & Taggart, R. *Jobs for the Disabled*. Washington, D.C.: George Washington University, Center for Manpower Policy Studies, 1976.

Martin, E. "New Public Priorities in Education of Handicapped Children." *Compact*, August 1974, pp. 4-7.

Olympus Research Corporation. *An Assessment of Vocational Education Programs for the Handicapped Under Part B of the 1968 Amendments to the Vocational Education Act*. Salt Lake City, 1974.

Phelps, L. A. and Halloran, W. D. "Assurance for Handicapped Learners: New Law Supports Expanded Role for Vocational Education." *American Vocational Journal* 51-8:36-7.

Phillips, L. *Barriers and Bridges*. California Advisory Council on Vocational Education, 1975.

President's Committee on Employment of the Handicapped. *Hiring the Handicapped: Facts and Myths*. Washington, D.C.: no date.

Tindall, L. W. "Education for All Handicapped Persons: A Mandate for the New Year." *American Vocational Journal* 53-1:26-29.

The Rehabilitation Act Amendments of 1974, Public Law 93-516. Washington, D.C.: U.S. Government Printing Office, 1974.

9

Equal Employment Opportunity Act: *Basic Human Rights and Responsibilities in the Work Place*

Objectives

- The student will describe some of the social forces which brought about the Civil Rights Act and the Equal Employment Opportunity Act.
- The student will describe how these legislative enactments have affected vocational education planning and programming.

Introduction

The original intent of the Civil Rights Act of 1964 and subsequent amendments was to provide equal employment opportunities to all groups by specifically forbidding an employer to limit, classify, or segregate employees in a way that would deprive any individual of employment opportunities. The Equal Employment Opportunity Act which is a part of the Civil Rights Act is an extremely comprehensive piece of legislation which has brought about continuous changes in employment practices. Further, litigation has continued to have an impact upon employment practices and to result in changes of rules and regulations pertaining to the Equal Employment Opportunity Act.

Because of the comprehensive nature of this legislation, a general overview will be discussed in this chapter rather than a detailed analysis of all facets of the act. Many of the provisions of the Civil Rights Act of 1964 and the Equal Employment Opportunity Act have been incorporated into the legislation discussed in the preceding chapters.

Laws and Enforcement Agencies

Fair employment practices, equal pay, seniority, hiring of the handicapped, and affirmative action programs will in most cases cause the working public to react in a variety of ways. Each of the above terms is a part of the effort of the federal government to insure that each individual, regardless of race, sex, religion, national origin, or handicap receives equal treatment in the world of work. This is a very complex area of human behavior and it is getting more complex and receiving more emphasis at the national, state, and local level as time goes on.

The first major laws were written in the early 1960s. The Civil Rights Act of 1964 and the Equal Employment Opportunity Commission, created under this act, were among the federal government's first major efforts to achieve nationwide fair employment practices. Other laws that deal with this subject have been passed, such as the Equal Pay Act of 1963, the Age Discrimination in Employment Act of 1967, the Rehabilitation Act of 1974 and the Equal Employment Act of 1972.

The following are provided as a brief overview of the various laws which are directed toward equal employment opportunity:

1. Title VII of the Civil Rights Act of 1964 as amended by the Equal Employment Opportunity Act of 1972
2. Presidential Executive Orders 11246, 11375, 11141, 11478, 11758
3. Equal Pay Act of 1963 as amended by the Education Amendments of 1972
4. Age Discrimination in Employment Act of 1967
5. Section 500 and 503 of the Rehabilitation Act Amendments of 1974
6. The National Labor Relations Act of 1947 as amended by the Labor-Management Reporting and Disclosure Act of 1959.

In most cases, state and local laws parallel federal legislation.

Two federal organizations have major responsibility for enforcement of the provisions of the Equal Employment Act and other related legislation. The Equal Employment Opportunity Commission, created under the Civil Rights Act of 1964, can take action against an employer, employment agency, labor organization, or joint labor-management committee controlling apprenticeship or other training or retraining, including on-the-job training, which is alleged to have engaged in unlawful employment practices.

The second major federal enforcement organization is the Office of Federal Contracts Compliance, which monitors affirmative action programs required by law. This office can take action against a company in which deficiencies are found to exist in affirmative action programs and hiring practices.

While the EEOC and the Office of Federal Contracts Compliance are the major agencies charged with the responsibility of insuring compliance with the various aspects of the Equal Employment Opportunity Act and related legislation, there are also numerous federal, state, and local agencies which enforce these laws.

A list of the various laws and executive orders and their enforcement agencies are provided here:

1. Title VII: Equal Employment Opportunity Commission (EEOC) (except for federal government action, which is enforced by the individual agencies, with final authority resting with the U.S. Civil Service Commission)
2. Executive Orders; Orders 11246, 11375: Office of Federal Contract Compliance (OFCC) and the contracting federal agencies. Order 11478: Individual agencies and U.S. Civil Service Commission.
3. Equal Pay Act: Wage and Hour Division of the U.S. Department of Labor.
4. Age Discrimination Act: Wage and Hour Division of the U.S. Office of Labor for Employers, Unions, Employment Agencies, and state and local governments
   Individual agencies and U.S. Civil Service Commission for federal government.
5. Rehabilitation Act and Executive Order 11758: Office of Federal Contract Compliance (OFCC), and to a minor extent, contracting agencies.
6. NLRA: National Labor Relations Board (Higgins, 1976)

One of the major problems facing the key enforcement agencies is a lack of available human resources. With a history of tight budgets for this particular phase of their operations, these agencies have not been able adequately to carry out their assignments. However, there appears to be a shift toward stronger enforcement of the provisions and a higher priority for the allocation of human resources to accomplish the objective of equal employment opportunity.

Equal Employment Opportunity and Affirmative Action

The Civil Rights Act of 1964 addressed five major issues: equal employment opportunity, voting rights, equal education, fair housing, and public accommodation. These problem areas have yet to be resolved completely. Equal Employment Opportunity is receiving considerable attention and at this time is having considerable impact upon the world of work and upon vocational education. Two major terms, EEO and Affirmative Action, are often used interchangably and are thought to mean the same thing. Equal Employment Opportunity means that everyone has an equal chance for employment based upon qualifications. The laws prohibit discrimination due to race, color, religion, sex, national origin, and handicap. These laws apply to all areas of employment including recruitment, hiring, training, promotion, job assignment, benefits, discipline, and discharge.

Affirmative Action, on the other hand, goes beyond EEO and requires the employer to make an extra effort to hire and promote members of the groups the laws were designed to protect, primarily minorities and females who wish to enter male-intensive occupations.

The laws are very complex and the agencies responsible for enforcement, have, over the years, placed varying degrees of emphasis on different requirements which make it difficult for companies, labor unions, vocational training institutions, and other training agencies to know if they are in compliance.

Planning for the future and the establishment of realistic goals to meet Affirmative Action and Equal Employment Opportunity requirements must begin with an analysis of the nation's work force, and a projection of the need for workers in the various occupational areas likely to be most affected. Local State Employment Security Agencies are to be utilized in securing the human resource information for Affirmative Action data. The primary focus of an analysis of employment practices for any company is upon underutilization or in some cases overutilization of females in certain jobs. Overutilization is viewed unfavorably because females and minorities are usually in low-paying, dead-end jobs. Efforts must be made, therefore, to train and promote these employees from the low-paying or dead-end jobs.

Another basic element in the Affirmative Action planning process is the time element. Goals and time tables must be established which are designed to overcome situations in previously identified areas where women and minorities have been underutilized. "Good faith efforts" include such things as recruitment, tuition assistance or refund programs, inservice or on-the-job training programs designed specifically for those individuals previously excluded from the higher paying jobs or occupations.

Recruitment is one of the first steps in a company's contact with potential employees. All phases of recruitment, from newspaper advertisements to the interviewing and selection procedure must be free of race and sex bias, and special efforts must be made to encourage minorities and females to apply. A similar requirement has been placed upon the recruitment of students for occupational education programs at all levels in secondary and postsecondary education. The primary intent in the latter case is to provide training for all persons; these in turn will be qualified to enter the labor market and assist business, industry, and labor to meet the requirements of Equal Employment Opportunity laws. Selection for hiring must be based upon qualifications, abilities, and potential. The selection criteria must be free of bias; if race, sex, handicap, or age are used as criteria for selection, then discrimination has occurred.

A further requirement of Equal Employment Opportunity legislation is the presence of support services to insure that once hired, these employees get the help they need to succeed. In other words, an employer can still be held liable for discriminatory acts of his or her employees done in the course of their duties. It appears that the intent of the 1976 vocational education act is the same as that of the EEO. That is, once recruited into traditionally male intensive vocational education programs, vocational teachers, counselors, and administrators must provide the help necessary for females, minorities, and the handicapped to succeed in their vocational programs.

Summary

The Civil Rights Act of 1964, and subsequent legislation deals with basic human rights and responsibilities in the work place. The primary purpose is to insure that each individual, regardless of race, sex, national origin, or handicap, will receive equal treatment and that selection for employment, education, apprenticeship, or membership in a labor organization will be based upon qualifications. As a result of affirmative action planning, employers must establish a system whereby inequities are removed.

This chapter has provided a brief overview of the legislation dealing with equal employment opportunity. Continued study of new rules and regulations and future legislation will reveal that we are probably seeing the beginning rather than the end of equal employment legislation and that considerable effort will be directed toward bringing about equity based upon qualifications.

Questions for Review

1. What are some of the major social forces that led to the enactment of the Equal Employment Opportunity Act?

2. What are the major problems faced by the enforcement agencies responsible for the Equal Employment Opportunity Act?

3. What implications do these legislative enactments have for recruitment of minorities, women, and handicapped individuals into vocational programs?

4. What are the differences between Equal Employment Opportunity and Affirmative Action?

Suggested Activities

1. Obtain a written Affirmative Action plan and review the provisions, with specific attention to recruitment of women and minorities in non-traditional jobs. Determine if these goals and objectives are realistic.

2. Develop a recruitment plan which will enable vocational administrators to increase the enrollment of females in male-intensive occupations or the enrollment of males in female-intensive occupations.

3. Survey a local vocational school to determine if the building is barrier free and that handicapped students have access to the vocational programs.

4. Interview the State Bureau of Vocational Education officer who has responsibility for elimination of sex stereotyping and for equity, to determine what plans have been implemented at the state level to comply with the above act.

Bibliography

Alper, S. W. "Racial Differences in Job and Work Environment." *Journal of Applied Psychology* 60(1): (1975):132-34.

Civil Rights Act of 1964. No. 701-716, p. 241. Pub. L. No. 88-352, 78 Stat. 241 (1964).

Equal Employment Opportunity Commission. *Guidelines on Employee Selection Procedures,* No. 1607 (35 FR 12333), August 1970.

Freeman, B. "Changes in the Labor Market for Blacks." *Brookings Papers on Economic Activity,* 1973, No. 1, pp. 67-131.

Glazer, N. *Affirmative Discrimination.* (New York: Basic Books, Inc., 1975).

Hamner, W., Kim, J. S., Baird, L. L., and Bigoness, W. J. "Race and Sex as Determinants of Ratings by Potential Employers in a Simulated Work Sampling Task." *Journal of Applied Psychology* 59(6) (1974):705-11.

Higgins, J. M. "A Manager's Guide to the Equal Employment Opportunity Laws." *Personnel Journal* 55 (August 1976):407.

Ledvinka, J. "Technical Implications of Equal Employment Law for Manpower Planning." *Personnel Psychology* 28(3) (1975):299-323.

Office of Federal Contract Compliance. *Affirmative Action Programs.* (36 Fr 23151), Dec. 1971, pp. 60-62.

Sovern, M. *Legal Restraints on Racial Discrimination in Employment.* New York: The Twentieth Century Fund, 1966.

Stanton, E. S. "The Discharged Employee and the EEO Laws." *Personnel Journal* 55 (March 1976):128.

Notes and Revisions

10

Future Trends: *How to Make That Educated Guess*

Objectives

- The student will review all manner of information concerned with pending occupational, vocational, or career education legislation.
- The student will identify major sources of current educational legislation information.
- The student will prepare a legislative blueprint (outline) describing a proposed enactment designed to promote current trends in occupational education.
- The student will develop and maintain an organizational diagram depicting the administrative structure for occupational education from the federal level through the local level. This diagram will contain the names of the various administrative personnel.

Introduction

Contemporary commentary regarding pending occupational education legislation is fraught with varying degrees of excitement and concern. Many occupational educators are excited over the possibility that proposed legislative enactments will provide increased funding for curriculum development and implementation as well as research. Many believe that these funds will be made available in a more efficient manner. On the other hand, some educators are concerned that much of the proposed educational legislation will have negative effects on their own propitious niche. However, far too many occupational education personnel are not familiar enough with various contemporary legislative proposals to make any judgments at all.

With increasing public concern over educational programs and resultant legislative moves, it is imperative that occupational educators and managers keep abreast of current legislative bills. Not only must these people be familiar with current legislative proposals, but, in order to arrive at decisions that will accurately reflect future trends, they must have the ability to analyze the effects on these proposals of current social, economic, political, and professional factors. Educational managers in the process of developing long- and intermediate-range program plans cannot rely on current priority and funding levels as indicators of the future. They must possess the ability to use current information to predict future program parameters that might develop.

Change has been the single most-significant aspect of educational legislation over the past decade. As previous chapters have indicated, not only have the individual enactments themselves changed, but interpretation within the framework of each Act is in a constant state of flux. Many of these interpretative changes occur primarily because of personnel shifts within the various agencies responsible for the administration of the enactment. For example, much of recent emphasis on career education came about because of Sidney P. Marland who, until recently, served as U.S. Commissioner of Education and who also was very interested in career education. In fact, much of the initial funding for career education research came from enactments in which the term "career education" did not exist.

Not only do individual personnel play an important role in the nature of legislation through the administrative branches, but their role also can greatly affect program change within the framework of an existing legislative enactment. For example, the level of appropriation for a specific Part of an enactment can vary from year to year. In fact, many laws provide for the authorization of monies for certain sections, while Congress may never appropriate funding to that Section of the Act (see Chapter 1, page 11). Hence, even after an Act is passed, legislative personnel can greatly affect the real nature of the Act.

Information Sources

It should be quite clear, even to the casual observer, that personnel responsible for local program decision making in occupational education must have available to them sources of information regarding pending legislation; current federal, state, and local administrative structures; and the philosophical orientation of various legislative and administrative personnel with regard to occupational education. Contrary to popular professional belief, this type of information is readily available.

Information regarding the status of pending enactments, as well as current appropriations for on-going legislative enactments, is available through various daily, weekly, and biweekly publications which may be found listed in the bibliography at the end of this chapter.

At the state level, weekly and monthly legislative digests are generally available to the public. These digests describe the status of various state legislative proposals and enactments.

National and state professional organizations generally provide legislative columns in their various publications. These columns describe the status of various pending enactments and, in many cases, provide information relative to the stance taken by legislators on the enactment.

Finally, most state and national representatives will provide, on a periodic basis, a newsletter describing their stand on critical issues of all types.

While some states are in the process of developing workable Management Information Systems that will provide much of the aforementioned kinds of information to the local education program director, specific information regarding local trends and political thought must be collected and analyzed by the occupational education program planner.

Summary

Legislative prognostication is an essential element in program planning. It requires a thorough knowledge of previous enactments and their effects on occupational programs at the local level. Also, it requires a thorough knowledge of current and pending enactments, their possible administrative procedures, and professional as well as lay public interpretation of their meanings.

In the end, the occupational education program manager must develop various plans based on a thorough analysis of existing trends. A valid analysis can come about only through an unbiased and systematic study of past enactments, current legislative proposals, and the personnel involved in both the preparation and administration of the various laws. Finally, the analysis must be tempered with an understanding of the social, political, and professional factors that continually affect all facets of the educational program.

Questions for Review

1. What will be the effects of such legislative proposals as educational revenue sharing, comprehensive manpower training, and voucher education on future occupational education legislation?

2. What will be the effect of career education concepts on future legislative enactments?

Suggested Activities

1. Prepare a legislative blueprint outlining a future enactment designed to promote current concepts in occupational or career education. See chapter 1 for description of a legislative blueprint.

2. Prepare a list of representatives and senators from your state. Analyze each individual with respect to past voting records on educational bills.

Bibliography

Please note that the bibliography for this chapter is of a general nature. It is designed as a source list for pertinent types of publications that provide, on a periodic basis, data useful in making that "educated guess" regarding future legislation. These are only some of the many available resources.

Burkett, Lowell A. "Latest Word From Washington." *American Vocational Journal.* Published monthly, September through May, by the American Vocational Association, 1510 H. St., N. W., Washington, D.C. 20005. Nonmember subscription rate is $4.00/year.

Education Daily. Published daily by Capitol Publications, Inc., Suite G-12, 2430 Pennsylvania Avenue, N. W., Washington, D.C. 20037. The annual subscription rate of this publication is $195.00.

Junior College Journal. Published monthly by the American Association of Junior Colleges. Subscription available at $5.00/year from Publisher Services, Inc., 621 Duke Street, Alexandria, Virginia 22314.

Kappan's Washington Bureau. "Washington Report." *Phi Delta Kappan.* Published monthly, September through June, by Phi Delta Kappa, Inc., 8th and Union, Bloomington, Indiana 47401. Nonmember subscription rate is $8.00/year.

Manpower and Vocational Education Weekly. Published weekly by Capitol Publications, Inc. (See *Education Daily* for address.) The annual subscription rate is $85.00.

Report on Education of the Disadvantaged. Published every other Wednesday by Capitol Publications, Inc. (See *Education Daily* for address.) The annual subscription rate is $40.00.

Many other publications, as mentioned earlier in this chapter also are useful. Due to their specific nature, however, it would be inappropriate to list them here.

Notes and Revisions